CW00833147

PROTECT YOURSELF!
A Woman's Handbook

Jessica Davies

PIATKUS

© 1990 Jessica Davies

First published in 1990 by
Judy Piatkus (Publishers) Ltd,
5 Windmill Street, London W1

British Library Cataloguing in Publication Data
Davies, Jessica
    Protect yourself : a handbook for women.
    1. Women. Self – defence
    I. Title
    613.66088042

    ISBN 0–7499–1005–4
        0–7499–1010–0 (Pbk)

Designed by Paul Saunders
Photography by Lucy Davies

Set in 11/13pt Linotron Plantin Light by
Phoenix Photosetting, Chatham, Kent
Printed and bound in Great Britain by
Bookcraft Ltd, Midsomer Norton, Avon

For my sister Lucy, and all my girlfriends

Acknowledgements

This book was made possible by the help of several people, without whom I would not have known where to start. I am indebted to PCs Brendan Brett and Alan Coles of the Crime Prevention Unit at Notting Hill police division, who advised me on all aspects of home and neighbourhood security; Mike Reed of Driving Management supplied expert tips for women drivers; Superintendent Ian Blair explained the current changes in police procedure. I am especially grateful to Clare Short MP for agreeing to write the foreword, and to Anna Raeburn and Chief Superintendent Clive Pearman for reading through the typescript and adding their own expert suggestions.

Finally, I would like to thank Clair Canning and Simon Hallgarten for demonstrating the moves in the photographic section, Corinne Hall for editing the book in its early stages, and Charles for his support and encouragement throughout the project.

Contents

Foreword

By Clare Short MP

It is sad that we need to discuss how to protect ourselves. But the truth is that almost all women feel scared at times. Like the author of this book, I look back at the things I did in my youth and feel worried for my former self! I am angry that I have lost that innocence and freedom. But there is no doubt I am worried when I walk home through dark streets late at night.

I am aware of course that the statistical chance of any one of us being attacked is small, and I keep telling myself and my friends that young males are more likely to be attacked in the streets at night. But my instincts tell me to be frightened. It was a woman who told me to cross over when male footsteps caused me to be worried. Before that I kept walking – grimly.

I was mugged, fairly recently, in a car park. He thumped me in the back and ran off with my bag. I bawled and shouted and chased him. He dropped the bag and a policeman heard my shouting and continued the chase. I got everything back and felt very proud of myself. It would have been devastating to lose my keys and diary and papers, and perhaps it was the loss of my constituency papers that made me brave. The experience has somehow made me less scared but more careful.

What is important is that we learn how to protect ourselves – and each other – without losing our freedom. That is what this book is about. Warnings that scare us make things worse. Sensible advice like this will make us brave and strong. I hope that by reading *Protect Yourself!*, you will grow in awareness and strength and demand the changes in society that will make us all safe.

Introduction

I was not an expert on self-protection when I started this book, and like most women had a haphazard approach to my personal security. Naturally I'd thought about it – grisly newspaper reports made sure of that – but never did I believe I would become a victim. I hitched lifts, I befriended strangers on late-night trains, I took short cuts when I knew the long way round was safer. You could say I was rightly living life to the full, refusing to be hemmed in on account of my sex. Or you could say that I took appalling risks and that I was lucky not to meet danger.

The truth lies somewhere in between. Even for the foolhardy, the chances of attack are slim. Whatever our impressions from the media might be, we are actually extremely unlikely to suffer violent assault. Most men deplore attacks on women and it is therefore unnecessary for us to diminish the quality of our lives through excessive anxiety and caution. By the same token, however, you or I might just be among those women who *are* attacked. It's then that we begin to ask ourselves if we might have prevented the ordeal, and how we might have defended ourselves better.

Protect Yourself! A Woman's Handbook aims to answer those questions, dealing specifically with attacks by strangers (violence and rape within the family is a different issue, which this book does not attempt to deal with). My starting-point is twofold – a belief in a woman's right to live freely and without fear, combined with a realistic view of the world's dangers.

While we must feel able to go about our business and pleasure with the confidence of a man, we must also accept that we face special threats.

Prevention is the key to self-protection, and thus the focus of this book. So many attacks might never have happened if a few basic precautions had been taken. These are practical, common-sense measures which can enhance rather than diminish your quality of life, for by adopting them you can rid yourself of fear. I should stress that failure to adopt preventive measures does not make the attack the victim's 'fault'. It never is.

Self-defence training is part of the preventive package. By being aware of ways in which you can defend yourself physically, you are arming yourself with a new confidence as well as that all-important alertness to danger. If you are attacked, however, you should not rely upon and automatically respond with violence. Unlike many writers on the subject of self-defence, I do not believe that a woman who has been surprised by an assault will instantly and successfully put into practice her evening classes in karate. Life isn't like that. If you *have* to fight, make it dirty, painful (for him) and then get away – the Appendix outlines the basic moves.

In the final count nobody, however 'expert', can give advice that is watertight in every situation – good self-protection and self-defence are whatever works for you at the time. There are as many different types of woman as there are attackers and attacks, and while a well-placed kick may work in one case, yelling 'Fire!' may work in another. Each of us has to make our own decision in the moment of attack.

What we can do is prepare women for that decision, show them the choices and get them thinking positively about the many ways in which they can protect themselves: women can be helped to 'unlearn' dangerously inappropriate responses (such as 'freezing'); they can be taught to identify the early signals of trouble; they can learn to have more control in a dangerous confrontation; women can be taught that they can snatch the advantage from their attacker and get away.

The aim of this book is to teach all those lessons. I want

women who have read it to feel they no longer need to be afraid. I want them to feel free to live full and independent lives. I want them to believe that should they ever have to face an attacker, they are now fully armed to protect themselves.

CHAPTER 1

Assertiveness: Your First Line of Defence

Assertiveness and self-protection

The image of the woman of the 1990s is one of independence and strength. Never before has she had so much confidence and control over her destiny, and never before has she asserted herself so successfully in the workplace as the respected equal of men.

For all these brave and wonderful steps forward she continues to live under the shadow of threatened attack. For all her toughness, she remains afraid to walk down a dark street on her own. Men are threatened and attacked, too, but they do not share the special, acute fears that any woman feels, irrespective of age or status, when she cuts down an alleyway, or enters an empty house on her own late at night.

Why is this still *so?*
One reason is that most women do not conform to the images thrust upon us by the media. Older generations know little of the independence of the nineties career girl, having been taught the traditional feminine way of dependence on a man for all things, including protection. When faced with violence, their natural reaction is passive, even defeatist – *there's no point fighting because he's going to win anyway.*

Such a response is shared by the majority of other women who, in spite of decades of feminism, retain a basic lack of confidence which assumes defeat in any violent confrontation.

Even those who are the genuine 1990s self-reliant women are prone to the same passivity – centuries of conditioning ensure that we are ill-prepared to respond assertively to violence.

Challenging and overturning that essentially feminine conditioning, learning to be assertive and self-reliant in our everyday life, is our first step towards an effective programme for self-protection.

This word 'assertive', which will be explored more fully later in this chapter, has nothing to do with being aggressive. Nor is it about being uncooperative and negative – although some people mistakenly assume this. It involves, quite simply, learning how to communicate your wishes clearly, taking initiatives, making decisions and assuming responsibility for and control over your life. You have a right to consider your needs, so don't reject that right simply because you have a problem with the word 'assertive'.

Through learning assertive habits in all areas of your life, you will automatically begin to adopt a more positive attitude to danger. You won't become a superwoman who can fight off gangs singlehanded, nor will you ever completely rid yourself of fear; all of us, whatever our age or level of fitness, experience moments of terrifying vulnerability. For those women living in notorious danger areas that terror is ever-present.

But by becoming more assertive you will acquire a new confidence and sense of power, which grows with every assertive act you perform. Walking down that dark street at night you will no longer be a fearful 'victim', but someone who knows where she's going and who won't be messed about with. When a stranger comes to the door, you will have the firmness to turn him away politely. When your car plays up and you find yourself stuck in the middle of nowhere, you will have a positive plan of action. And when you have to negotiate the no-man's-land of an inner city estate, you will know that you have resources within you to call upon.

In every situation you will exude self-confidence and that, in turn, will make others respect you. You can't fake self-confidence – it must come from within you. This chapter will show you ways in which you can build self-confidence.

How assertive are you in everyday life?

Before going any further, you should look long and hard at your own patterns of behaviour. Remember, if you can't act positively in ordinary situations, you have little hope of springing into action in a time of crisis. Ask yourself a few questions:

- Are you someone who avoids confrontation at any cost? If you are, you lack assertiveness.
- Do you rely on others to sort out unpleasant situations on your behalf? If you do, you lack assertiveness.
- Or have you mastered the art of speaking your mind – however difficult that may be – pleasantly but firmly? If you have, you have developed an assertive attitude.

Jane was made aware of her own unwillingness to be assertive while she was working in the library. She was disturbed by the noisy arrival of three teenage girls who sat down near her, talking and laughing, slamming books on the table and then plugging into their Walkmans. These must have been on at full volume, for even readers at the far end of the library sighed loudly, shot them venomous looks . . . but then meekly returned to their studies.

Jane was seething. The metallic clanking escaping from the headphones inspired in her a cocktail of emotions – irritation, resentment and that familiar sense of anxiety: *should she confront them, or should she passively let them get away with their anti-social behaviour?* She is not an unassertive person, but this was a fearsome trio sporting bleached and spiked hairdos, leathers and kohl-streaked eyes, so her initial instinct was to leave them be. After all, she didn't want the aggravation of a fight, and if it all got too much, she argued, she could always go home.

Sneakily, she hoped the man sitting next to her would deal with the problem.

He didn't, and Jane's anger eventually got the better of her. She approached the girls and politely (but firmly) asked them to switch off their music. They laughed in her face and told her to get lost. There followed a strange battle of wills, wherein they continued to abuse her while she stood her ground and repeated her request. Suddenly it was over and Jane had won. Her refusal to budge must have embarrassed them into surly submission. Whatever, the clanking ceased and she returned to her seat. For a while, further rude comments were thrown her way, accompanied by guffaws of laughter, but this soon died out. She says she felt marvellous, powerful, unassailable.

The 'nice girl' syndrome

I recite the above anecdote because it illustrates the message of this book: *women have the right and the ability to act assertively when confronted with a situation they do not like.* All we lack is the habit, and we are therefore ill-prepared to cope with harassment – verbal and physical – or, more crucially, violent attack.

Given the way we are raised, it's not too surprising. We are taught from birth that to be feminine is to be gentle, to be sweet-natured, to be giving, to be polite, to be non-confrontational. While these may sound an attractive set of virtues, they can be quite suicidal when, as an extreme example, we come fact to face with a sexual pervert. Our primal instincts may be flashing a red alert, but we override the warnings so as not to offend. At a harmless but exasperating level this might mean ignoring loud individuals in the library, but at the other end of the scale, it might mean admitting to your house a stranger who claims he is from the council or the gas board, but who bears no ID.

Only when it is too late do you realise that 'being nice' can be a treacherous business.

The habit of good manners, of never wishing to offend, is an especially feminine trait, and it frequently results in a passive response to danger. This renders us uniquely vulnerable. Our awareness of that vulnerability makes us fearful, and thrusts us further into 'victim' mentality. It's a vicious circle which the attacker exploits.

Living in fear – how the media present us

The image of female vulnerability is reinforced by the media and this enhances the climate of fear. In fact, the vast majority of criminal acts are against property, with less than 5 per cent of recorded crime being against people. And seven out of ten violent assaults are on men (although one should treat these figures with caution, as they also include young men who become involved in pub brawls and so forth). Yet the reports splashed across our newspapers are so often of the hideous one-off atrocities, brutal sexual attacks on women.

The paradox is that while such attacks make the news because of their relative rarity, we actually come to believe that they are regular events because we keep reading about them in the papers. This distorted perception of reality can have three very negative effects on women:

- It can force us to hem in our lifestyle unnecessarily.
- It can convince us that we truly are victims.
- This conviction leads us to freeze and/or give in under attack.

None of this is necessary.

Movies and the world of fiction don't do us many favours either. Time and again we have watched the hackneyed image of the defenceless female attacked by a hooded stranger in the dark of night. If she's lucky, a man – any man! – may rescue her from the jaws of rape or death. Whatever her fate, you can be sure she will prove herself helpless and at the mercy of her assailant. In the more grotesque versions of this tale, the implication will be that she is, in some way, enjoying the assault.

The recurrent message that we are weak and defenceless has the dual effect of sapping our confidence in our ability to protect ourselves, and of peopling our world with vicious bogeymen.

A positive approach to fear

The fear to which so many of us have become accustomed, and which undermines the quality of our lives, is born very largely of these warped images and not of reality. Imagine how that fear would be reduced if the movie images were of strong women putting up a fight, and if the newspaper stories were of the scores of women who have struggled and got away from their aggressors. It does happen, and often – as the excellent book *Her Wits About Her* edited by Denise Caignon and Gail Groves (The Women's Press) testifies. Here, survivors of violent assaults recount how they escaped, and one tale that sticks in my memory goes like this:

> *Rapist*: 'I'm going to rape you.'
> *Woman*: 'Oh no you're not.'
> *Rapist*: 'I guess you're right.'

He doesn't.

Another reassuring story is that of Susan Davis, which was reported in the press in January 1990:

> Susan was pounced upon by a youth who shouted obscenities, punched her face and tore her clothes before pinning her against a wall and threatening to rape her. She fought back, and after a violent struggle, managed to hold on to 17-year-old John Stevens until a neighbour was able to summon help.
>
> After being awarded £250 in court for her courage she's reported to have said: 'I couldn't believe his change of personality. He became meek and mild and kept saying "What will my mum and dad say? *Please let me go.*" Then he said he wouldn't be able to afford a fine. I was astonished that after what he did to me he thought he was going to get off with a fine.'
>
> Susan then went on to make a vital point: 'I did what all women should do when a man invades their body. Most sex attackers are insignificant weeds which is why they do this sort of thing.'

What is the typical attacker like?

All attackers are different, and you cannot be sure that yours isn't that very rare beast – a psychopath. However, most attackers (whether their intention is to grab your handbag or to rape you) are opportunists who don't want you to cause any trouble. Their greatest advantage is the element of surprise and the resultant freezing or passive response they expect from you. If you disprove that model of behaviour, you will surprise them and gain an advantage. Their priority may now switch from attack to escape – they don't want trouble.

The slim likelihood of attack

You are in fact extremely unlikely to be attacked at all, and even less likely to suffer at the hands of a stranger – some two-thirds of assaults on women are committed by family, friends or acquaintances. Although this knowledge may be of little comfort to those who have experienced violence at the hands of a man they know, it helps provide a realistic perspective on the problem.

Hooded psychopaths are – mercifully – few and far between.

While it is impossible to produce wholly accurate figures for the frequency of incidents involving women victims (sexual assaults, in particular, are notoriously under-reported), and thereby assess the exact likelihood of any one woman becoming a victim, it *is* possible to make informed guesstimates.

Taking rape as an example, some 1000 rapes are reported in London each year. The estimated level of reporting varies from one in four to one in twelve. Even working from the worst of these figures – i.e., assuming that 12,000 rapes occur each year – we are still talking about a small minority of victims, 0.17 per cent of the 7 million women who live in or pass through London every year.

Superintendent Ian Blair, Deputy Chair of the Metropolitan Police Standing Committee on Serious Sexual Assault Against Adults, believes the real rape figure to be nearer 4000, which would mean the percentage of women suffering an attack in London drops to 0.056 per cent. Elsewhere in Britain this likelihood is significantly reduced.

I should stress that even if there were only one attack per

year, it would still be one attack too many – and *you* could be that victim. However, it's important that women realise that the problem is perhaps not as bad as many of us perceive it to be.

Putting your fear in perspective and regaining control

A survey in *Company* magazine gives a good indication of how much our fear exceeds the likelihood of anything actually happening. Out of 5000 respondents, as many as 93 per cent worried about going out alone after dark, while 90 per cent would simply not go out if it meant travelling home alone at night.

It is clearly not right for women to be scared off the streets by their fear of attack.

- Why should we not enjoy the same freedom as men to move about on business and pleasure?
- Why should we feel powerless in the face of dark and unspecified dangers?
- Why should we have to tolerate that clammy sense of rising panic when we return to our homes or our cars at night, when we wait at a deserted bus stop, when we have to work late at the office and alone?

Banishing the received images of the woman-victim and recognising the unlikelihood of our becoming one is the first step towards liberating ourselves from fear – *and by this I do not advocate a cavalier attitude to danger, for it is there and we must all be aware of it.*

What we are doing is transforming our unspecified fear of 'what might happen' into something more useful: an awareness that there is a problem, but that it is one with which we can deal.

Next, we must banish the received images of the sinister, hooded and maniacal attacker. As I have already mentioned, most attacks are made by men known to the victim. Furthermore, the vast majority of men who prey upon women are looking for an easy target, and will back off if their intended victim becomes troublesome. They are, in short, cowards – just as Susan Davis said (see page 19).

Here is another case history to illustrate this point:

> While out jogging, Fiona found that she was being followed. She tried to shake the man off, but in the end simply turned round and swore at him furiously, commanding him to leave her alone. He swore back and then turned away. She continued with her run, slightly shaken but thoroughly pleased with herself for asserting her right to be alone.

I'll never forget the delight with which Fiona told me of this victory. I am not advocating a casual approach to the threat of attack. What I am saying is that we need to kill off the myths about pathetic women victims and unbeatable bogeymen before we do anything else.

Assertiveness as a way of life

Fiona's rage is really the key to the conquest of those twin enemies of safety and well-being: our fear and our habit of being 'nice'. By admitting and expressing our anger we are stating positively our refusal to accept imposed limits on our life. We are demanding respect and declaring uncompromisingly that we will not be seen as victims. These are skills we all need to learn – whatever our age or circumstances.

For some women this may seem a very tall order, especially those brought up in earlier generations, where traditional feminine behaviour was the order of the day. Anger is something many of us have learned to suppress, and if you are used to deferring to others in everyday life, you are unlikely to become a fearsome lioness in a time of crisis. Very many women see themselves as programmed to accept the decisions and actions of others, especially men.

The trouble is, that's the way an attacker will see them too.

If at this point you are saying, 'Well, she's not talking about me – *I'm* forthright and assertive, and I don't let others trample on me,' ask yourself a few questions:

- If someone comes into the non-smoking carriage of the train and lights up, do you ask them to stub out their cigarette?
- If the gasman comes, mends your boiler and then overcharges you, do you fight your corner?
- If a salesman comes to your door, do you firmly tell him that you are not interested?
- If your bottom is pinched in a crowded bus, do you try to identify the pest and announce what he's done to everyone else?
- If you are followed or flashed at, do you express your outrage and then report the incident – however 'minor' – to the police?
- Or, on a different level, if your partner wants to make love and you don't, do you none the less give in to his demands so as to keep the peace?

If you can answer 'yes' to the first five of these questions, and 'no' to the last, you can skip the rest of this chapter. The chances are, however, that you will at least recognise the anxiety and indecision most of us feel in these and other situations, the self-doubt (did it really happen? am I being silly?), the guilt (did I invite this in some way?) and the instinct to do anything but make a fuss.

Assertiveness versus aggression

Contrary to what many of us believe, being assertive isn't in fact about 'making a fuss'. Our culture has bestowed on all of us a complex jumble of ideas about how we should behave, and even those of us who see ourselves as strong and emancipated drag around a damaging baggage of notions. Assertiveness, especially in a woman, is frequently confused with aggression, and, as we've all been told from birth, an aggressive woman is not an appealing one. It's vital that we don't allow this misconception to prevent us from learning assertive habits.

Bearing in mind that an assertive approach in everyday life is the first step towards assertiveness under attack, consider the difference between the two approaches below:

Catherine has bought a jumper, only to discover after one wear that a seam has come loose. She storms back to the shop, and *aggressively* demands a refund.

Catherine: 'I've worn this jumper once and it's already falling apart. I'm sick of your shoddy goods, and I want my money back.'

Assistant: 'I'm sorry, it's not our policy to give refunds on goods that have been worn.'

Catherine: 'I don't give a damn about your policy. I want my money back.'

Assistant: 'I can't do that for you. Now, perhaps you could let me serve this lady behind you.'

The conversion could go on like this indefinitely, with each of the players adopting an increasingly entrenched position. If you were the sales assistant, would you want to bend the rules for someone like Catherine? If, on the other hand, she were to adopt an *assertive* approach, the scene might go like this:

Catherine: 'I've worn this jumper once and it's already falling apart. I'd be grateful if you could give me a refund – I have my receipt here.'

Assistant: 'I'm sorry, it's not our policy to give refunds on goods that have been worn.'

Catherine: 'I understand your position, but I'd be grateful if you could refund me my money none the less.'

Assistant: 'Well, I'll have to talk to my manager . . .'

Catherine: 'That's fine. I'll wait here if you could go and do that now . . .'

Are assertiveness and aggression really the same thing? It's not hard to see which approach achieves better results with the minimum of stress. Don't be put off by confusing assertiveness with aggression – they are very different things.

What is so important about learning assertiveness in every-day life is that it gives you a control and a confidence in a whole range of situations, which give you an advantage over

the aggressive person. You learn to value yourself and your judgement, and these lessons are invaluable when you are threatened.

Assertiveness versus passive resentment

An alternative to aggression or assertiveness is the more covert approach, where we smother our ill-feeling. Beneath the smiling exterior, we store up our resentment, which can be as bad for us as it is for the people around us.

Imagine the case of a young professional woman called Alice.

On the way to work, Alice is leered and whistled at by a gang of workmen. The attention is unwanted and makes her feel uncomfortable – it happens every day, and every day she tries to ignore it. At lunchtime, she goes to the canteen with a male colleague. One steak remains and she really wants it, but she knows that he does, too, so she goes for the salad instead, persuading herself that it's better for her figure anyway.

Late that afternoon, her boss asks her to stay on after hours for a meeting. Actually, she's committed to a date with an old friend who's going through a rough time at the moment, but Alice is anxious to appear willing so she cancels the friend. She arrives home tired and hungry. The flat's a mess and although her husband has been back for two hours, he's prepared no food and is relaxed in front of the TV. She puts the dinner in the oven, tidies up while it cooks, serves it and washes up.

This example is by no means extreme, and there will be elements with which all of us can identify. The effect on Alice of her actions will be feelings of:

● guilt
● resentment
● lack of control over her life
● loss of confidence and self-esteem.

With some women, this may erupt in aggressive behaviour – shouting at the workmen, for example, in a manner that will only encourage further irritating harassment. In others, it will emerge more covertly – sarcastic remarks as a way of indicating to the husband that his behaviour is not on. Neither of these approaches will solve Alice's problems or make her feel any better.

Wouldn't a direct, assertive approach be much more positive? In the case of Alice, her day might look quite different, and she would certainly feel a whole lot better if she only grasped the nettle assertively each time she found herself being forced into a role she didn't like.

Here's how she might deal with her day – assertively:

With the workmen she might try saying something like, 'Please don't whistle/talk to me like that. I know you think it's harmless fun, but I find it offensive.' The lunchtime steak is less straightforward. But she could state that she'd like it, recognise that her colleague might too, and then suggest, perhaps, that they share it and the salad.

This may sound slightly absurd to most women whose instinct is not to make an issue over small matters. But if you think about it, why should Alice and her ilk always make the sacrifices that others will never make for her? Why must her needs always come after those of others? Later in the day, when Alice's boss makes the request for that meeting, she could respond by explaining that she has an important prior engagement which she is unable to cancel, but that she'd be willing, for example, to come in early the following morning.

Here, negotiation is the crucial point. Alice offers an alternative and proves that she is both in control and willing. Back at home, she could tell her husband how tired and hungry she is, and ask him to make dinner and share the chores. Like a lot of people (men and women alike), he is also tired at the end of the day and will happily let someone else do the work if he can get away with it. It's her responsibility to ensure he knows he can't.

Told in this way it all sounds so easy, which of course it isn't. For most women, all of those situations will have been bound up with feelings of guilt and indecision. It *is* hard for people to change the habits of a lifetime, and even harder to change your basic personality. However, it is possible, through practice, to acquire a more assertive attitude. In doing so, your self-confidence grows and you begin to feel able to cope with situations that would have floored you in the past.

The later chapters in this book will demonstrate how this new self-confidence can protect you when in danger.

How do you begin to change your unassertive ways?

We all have to begin at the beginning if we're going to achieve that positive frame of mind. You will only react assertively under attack if you have the confidence that assertiveness in other areas of your life will have given you – remember, you're unlikely to become a lioness under threat, when your usual approach to life is mouse-like.

A very good and well-established way of starting out involves writing a list of situations in which you would like to be more forceful. These might include, for example:

a. Telling your flatmate/partner that they aren't doing their share of housework.

b. Telling your sister that you don't have the time to babysit every Tuesday.

c. Asking your neighbours not to play loud music so late at night.

d. Telling your family that you won't be coming home for Christmas this year.

e. Telling a demanding friend that you can't go on giving them so much of your time.

f. Saying 'no' to people who want to smoke in your house.

g. Saying 'no' to the choir committee who want you as chairperson next year – you haven't the time.

h. Complaining to your car dealer about the problems you've had with your vehicle, and insisting he pay for repairs.

27

You should tackle the list from the bottom upwards, starting with the least formidable situation first, and working your way up to the most difficult one. If you dive straight in at the deep end, you risk discouragement and defeat before you've even begun. If, on the other hand, you start with the easier challenges, you can build your confidence gradually.

So, taking the above list, you might begin with h, and work your way through to b or e – any situation which involves a close personal relationship is bound to throw up extra complications, and make greater demands on you. But don't let that deter you: in the long run, the relationship will be far more healthy when you aren't harbouring resentment.

The mechanics of assertiveness

Assertive behaviour is not a magical gift bestowed on some people alone. It's a skill which all of us are capable of mastering – irrespective of sex or personality type – so long as we learn the basic techniques.

Learning to be assertive means learning to recognise and tell others what it is that YOU want. It is therefore essential that in any situation you should begin by being absolutely clear in your own mind as to what that is – and that isn't always so easy. You may have acquired a habit of automatically thinking of others whenever presented with a choice, and this will blunt your ability to cut through to your wishes.

At the outset, you have to retrain yourself into acknowledging that you, like everybody else, have the right to make your feelings known, and to have those feelings respected.

Start listening to your intuition – it is one of your greatest gifts as a woman. To illustrate the point, imagine the following situation:

> Some close friends invite you for dinner, and you know that this week you really need an evening to yourself. What do you do?
>
> Normally, you might accept, and then worry about how you're going to get through the chores that have piled up at

home. But what about the assertive option? Here, you recognise your own needs and act accordingly: 'Thank you so much for asking me, but I'm afraid I can't make it.' Unless your friends are inordinately nosy, they are unlikely to press for further excuses. If they do, be honest and tell them that you are really bogged down. If you feel that's not enough, why not suggest they come round to you the following week when you have less on? Finally, if you are not quite sure what you really want, give yourself some time before committing yourself – 'Thank you for asking me. Can I let you know tomorrow, when I have an idea of my commitments?'

Stick with your decisions

Once you have made up your mind, stick with your decision and don't be swayed or forced to give in – this only invites a return of the guilt and resentment you have expelled with your assertiveness. The enemy to watch out for here is compassion, the feeling that you are letting others down by your decision. If you sense it creeping up on you, remind yourself that you have the absolute right to decide how you spend your time. And whatever you do, don't dress your words up in apologies and excuses, for they merely serve to confuse the listener and blunt your conviction.

The following example illustrates how once these techniques have become habit in everyday situations, they can be applied to one that is potentially dangerous:

It's late at night, and Sarah is on her own at home. The doorbell rings, and she opens it – using the security chain – to find a man on her doorstep.

Man: 'My car's stuck on the hill. Do you mind if I come in for a minute to make a phone call?'

Sarah hesitates. It's raining and she feels sorry for the man. But she doesn't know him, and her gut feeling is not to let him through the door.

Sarah: 'If you'd like to give me the number, I'd be happy to make the call for you.'

Man: 'Oh come on, it's wet out here. I'm not going to hurt you. Just let me in. I won't be long.'

Sarah (politely, but firmly sticking to her decision): 'Give me the number and I'd be happy to make the call for you.'

Man (getting angry): 'Look, I don't know what your problem is, but I think you're being paranoid.'

Sarah: 'You may think that, but I'm not letting you in the house. As I said, I'll make the call for you.'

The man may continue to get angry, or he may try other techniques – wheedling, arguing, trying to persuade. But so long as Sarah sticks by her initial statement, repeating and refusing to weaken or compromise, he will eventually get the message.

But, you may ask, is it really necessary to leave the poor fellow in the rain? He may be totally harmless. The answer to that one is, I'm afraid, an unequivocal 'Yes'.

Most men are appalled at the thought of violence to women, but it's never worth taking the risk. The one who pitches up on *your* doorstep could be the rare and nasty exception.

Assertive body language

Your positive words are as nothing if they are undermined by inappropriate body language. If you are going to speak your mind clearly, you have to reinforce your words with appropriate gestures and in the right tone of voice. Failure to do so will only serve to confuse or contradict your message. Imagine how smiles and an overtly 'feminine' manner would undermine the scene described above. The lines of communication have to be kept absolutely clear.

Assertive body language is an essential part of our self-defence armoury, and yet it's one of the hardest tricks for us to master. For a start, we habitually smile, and often at the least appropriate moments. If you doubt this, think about the times you have smiled sweetly when inside you've been boiling with suppressed rage. How many men do you know who adopt the same tactic? If you're still not convinced, look through a few photographs and you'll soon see that the broadest smiles are on the female faces.

But it's not just the smile that we get wrong. We twiddle our fingers and our hair, we stoop, we shuffle our feet, we fail to look our interlocutor in the eye and we slip into a coy sexual mode when we're trying to be taken seriously. Of course, a lot of men also reveal by their body language signs of nervousness, embarrassment, insecurity and so forth, but somehow it seems to be a failing to which women are especially prone, and once more, the habit stems from our programmed desire to be polite and lovable.

Where self-protection is concerned this is a disaster. It is well-established that attackers will prey on those who have 'victim' stamped on them. They don't want trouble, so they pick the women who look as though they won't give them any. By contrast, women who display confidence and an air of assertiveness will make them think twice.

Try looking at yourself, and identifying which of the good and which of the bad habits are yours:

Good (assertive) habits	Bad (unassertive) habits
Erect, relaxed posture, with head and shoulders held straight	Slouching, hunched posture
Balanced posture	Weight on one leg
Confident march	Apologetic shuffle
Relaxed and open eye contact	Shifty, nervous eye contact
Relaxed facial expression	Quick and nervous smile or tense brow, blushing
Voice firm and even-toned	Voice high, or very quiet, or uncertain, or mumbling
Casual hand movements – hands open and relaxed	Hands clenched or fiddling with hair, clothing, etc.

| Keeping a comfortable distance between yourself and the other person | Allowing the other person to get too close |

Once you've established your weak points, start working on them one by one, and you'll soon produce a dramatic change in the visual impression you project. Walking with your head held high actually makes you feel confident, and you'll find that by the simple process of altering your movements, gestures and your manner of speaking, you're also boosting your confidence.

If you find it hard to identify your own problem areas (and looking in a mirror can be more of a hindrance than a help!) why not join forces with a friend? Look at each other critically, and discuss together the ways in which each of you can harden up the signals you give out via body language. You're more likely to benefit from this exercise if you choose someone at your 'level', and not someone who is either substantially more or less proficient than you in these matters.

Conclusion: applying assertiveness to self-protection

By adopting an assertive atittude, you are telling the world that you are someone to be reckoned with. You are someone who knows your own mind. You are someone who will stand up for yourself. You are someone who will not bow to the wishes of others if they aren't compatible with yours. You are someone who is NOT a victim.

Assertiveness can never offer you 100 per cent protection, but nor can anything or anybody else. What it does is provide you with a positive and self-reliant approach to life which enables you to:

• Banish the bogeymen and eliminate the fear of imagined danger.
• Realistically assess and confront the potential danger in any situation.
• Take the necessary precautions, as described in the following chapters.

- Carry on a free and independent existence, confident that you have taken steps to protect yourself.

Much of the advice given in the pages that follow relies on an assertive attitude, and this applies especially where I am dealing with actual confrontation with danger. It is therefore essential that you examine your approach to life and actively seek to become more assertive in all ways. The work you put in here will serve as the bedrock for your self-protection programme.

In this chapter, my aim has been to explain the importance of assertiveness to self-protection. It is the foundation on which every woman should build her self-protection strategy. Many women may feel unable to develop assertiveness skills on their own, and they should contact the Redwood Women's Training Association which provides courses in assertion training and sexuality. The address is supplied on page 137.

A note on fitness

There are many other ways in which we can build up our level of confidence. Exercise comes top of the list, and it's something all of us should include in our daily routine, whatever our age. By improving your level of fitness, you'll sharpen your responses and build up a new body-awareness which will give you confidence in any dangerous situation.

Many women opt for martial arts courses – karate, aikido, judo and so on. The benefit here is the increased fitness and alertness you can acquire through hard training, rather than the ability to throw an assailant over your shoulder – this point is discussed later in Chapter 6. Contact addresses are supplied at the back of the book, along with suggested reading for those who wish to learn more about assertiveness.

Summary

These are the basic principles of the assertive way:

- Recognise that you have the right to decide in every situation what it is that YOU want.

- Listen to your intuition and allow it to tell you what it is that you want.

- Do not sublimate your feelings/wishes because you feel guilty or compassionate – learn to be angry.

- Do not let others persuade you to act against your wishes.

- State what you want clearly.

- Stick by your argument and repeat it if necessary.

- Back up your words with assertive body language.

CHAPTER 2

Getting Streetwise

Looking after yourself

This chapter and the three that follow it, deal with *avoidance* strategies. 'Getting Streetwise' addresses not only the problem of looking after yourself when you're out and about and on foot, it also examines the more general 'streetwise techniques' which apply in the later chapters.

Criminals of every category rely on opportunity, and it therefore makes sense to try to reduce that opportunity where you can. You are in danger if you do not learn to identify danger, and if you take no steps whatsoever to protect yourself. It is your responsibility to develop a strategy for your own personal safety as well as that of your children.

Some women may contest these views. Should the onus really be on us to prevent violence? By saying that we are responsible for reducing the likelihood of attack, am I not also suggesting that violent men cannot help their violent instincts? And therefore am I not, by inference, attaching a degree of 'blame' to victims of rape and muggings (had the victim looked after herself she would not have got in trouble etc., etc.)? Isn't it up to the men – not us – to change their ways?

Yes it is, of course. Generations of judges have done gross disservice to society by dealing leniently with sex offenders, excusing their behaviour as 'normal', if extreme. Only recently, in a case where a teenage girl was stripped and mauled by a gang of youths, the judge ruled that the attack was prompted by 'youthful high spirits'. The gang walked free from the court. The girl became a prisoner in her own home, afraid to go out and afraid to be alone with any man – even her own father.

If you start accepting violent behaviour as a natural male impulse, you are saying that it is, in effect, 'OK', and you are heading down a road which ends in the obscene suggestion that rape is natural, that the victim invited it, and that she even enjoyed it.

Men must be held responsible for their acts of violence against women and children. This does not, however, mean that potential victims cannot and should not adopt measures to protect themselves and their families. We're dealing with reality here, not sexual politics. Look at it this way: you may be an excellent driver, but that doesn't stop you from fastening your seat belt to protect yourself from the unpredictable behaviour of others.

Developing a useful awareness of danger

Being aware of the potential for danger is the vital starting-point. This was highlighted in a report commissioned by the Suzy Lamplugh Trust on the problem of violence at work: 70 per cent of the respondents listed awareness training as their top priority. Knowing your enemy enables you to erect appropriate defences. And if, in spite of your precautions, you are attacked, your process of psychological healing will be aided very significantly by the knowledge that you did everything you could to help yourself. Countless victims have tortured themselves with thoughts of how they might have escaped if they'd only taken some basic precautions.

The following example illustrates how you can get caught out if you don't open your eyes and consider IN ADVANCE the potential for danger in any situation.

Clare works in London and has just moved to a new house in the suburbs. Normally, her journey home poses no problem. She travels back by train with the commuters and then catches a bus which stops at the end of her street. One day, however, she has to work late. The bus service stops at 10 p.m. and by the time she reaches her home station, the last one is long gone. She faces a fifteen-minute walk home – she'd be happier getting a cab, but she's out of cash.

The quickest route takes her along the main road, through the park and into town. It's 11.30 p.m. and, as she sets off up the road, the street lights switch off. She'd always assumed they were on all night. Although she knows her way, she realises that she hasn't ever thought about its hazards, and she now feels nervous. Even though this is the quickest route, is it the safest at night? Is there an alternative way to go? Does she really have to cut through the park? It's too dark to work out the alternatives. *If only she'd thought it all through in advance. . .*

Having been through this experience Clare may decide never again to catch the late train, thus allowing her fear to impose unreasonable limits on her freedom of movement. Sadly, it's a choice many women will make.

On the other hand, she may use the experience to prepare herself mentally for the next time she gets the late train home. She will not be forced into cutting back her activities, but nor is she prepared to endure again the fear of that first journey. What she must do, then, is examine the circumstances, and work out some way of living with them:

- Does she really have to walk?
- Shouldn't she always make sure she has some change for a cab, in case she is unexpectedly delayed?
- Is there anyone she could call for a lift in an emergency?

If she *does* decide to walk:

- Is there a safer, better-lit route?
- Is there an alternative to the short cut through the park?
- What are the avenues of flight?
- Where is the nearest phone should trouble arise?

The simple exercise of addressing these questions will calm her fear of the unknown, and provide her with a clearer picture of the problem she has to deal with. It will also throw up practical antidotes to the threat of danger. She is *aware* of what that particular late night walk involves. She can now formulate a realistic plan for dealing with it.

Tactical precautions

Everyone has to establish her own level of what is acceptable. While one woman will decide that, in the end, she would rather pay for a cab on the occasions she faces a walk like Clare's, another will decide that the walk is quite safe – so long as she takes precautions.

By the same token, each one of us has to decide which precautions are appropriate and acceptable to us. Self-protection is a personal matter, and in the end, only you can decide what is best for you.

Remember that your precautions are not there further to limit your freedom. They are there to give you increased control over your life and movements.

In a situation like Clare's, where you are walking home late at night, some basic steps apply across the board:

- Plan your route in advance.
- Familiarise yourself with your route so that you know, for example, where there are large bushes or concealed entrances, and where your nearest points of help are (shops, pubs, phones, etc.).
- Vary your route if it's one you take frequently, so that your movements are less predictable.
- Think about escape routes.
- Keep to well-lit streets where possible.
- Avoid short cuts if you know the longer route is safer.
- Avoid pedestrian underpasses where possible.
- Avoid cutting through parks and car parks – both provide the isolation and the hiding places a would-be attacker loves.

- Keep to the outside of the pavement, so that it is harder for an attacker to spring from a doorway or alleyway; walk in the middle of the road if traffic permits.
- Walk towards oncoming traffic.
- Don't wear a Walkman – you need the use of all of your senses.
- Never accept a lift from a stranger, no matter how tempting it might seem.
- If someone is expecting you at your destination, call them before you set off, and let them know what time you expect to arrive.

Specific situations will call upon other, more specific, steps. The examples below should demonstrate that self-protection is largely a matter of common sense:
If you're out jogging or on a walk:

- Avoid isolated areas where possible.
- Tell someone at home where you're going, and how long you'll be.
- Never wear a Walkman.
- Take a dog with you if you can – or a friend!

If you're going to an unfamiliar neighbourhood:

- Try to plan your route in advance. Either refer to a map, or telephone whoever you are visiting for detailed instructions.
- Let someone know when you set off and when you expect to arrive.
- Walk purposefully, and look as if you know where you are going.
- Try to avoid referring to your map in deserted places. If you have to consult your map/instructions, try to do so in a public place, such as a shop.

If you're in a familiar neighbourhood:

- Don't forget that it could still be dangerous. Be on the alert all the time.

And wherever you might be, keep a close watch on your handbag and other personal possessions – don't make things easy for a thief.

- Try and keep shopping bags, etc. to a minimum.
- Carry in your bag only what you need – not the kitchen sink!
- Transfer keys and some cash into a pocket – it's safer.
- Have the flap pressed against your body, and keep a hand on the bag if you can.
- Wear your bag across your body. Don't leave it to dangle vulnerably on your shoulder.
- Avoid digging for things in your bag in the street.

The effectiveness of all of these tactics relies on *consistently* maintaining a high level of awareness whenever you are in a potentially dangerous situation, and on *consistently* thinking about your self-protection. Clare can only protect herself if she employs her chosen strategies *every time* she makes that walk home in the dark. The one night she wanders home with her head in the clouds may be the one night that she comes face to face with danger. Many women I have spoken to have listed a variety of effective and imaginative tactics of their own, but they have also confessed that they employ them only sporadically.

Learning to react positively to warning lights

Always being on the alert is not the same as always being fearful and jittery. It's about eliminating imagined dangers and using your fear positively to protect yourself.

Most of us don't realise that fear is actually a very good weapon. It's an intuitive reaction to danger, but one that we often fail to act upon. Imagine a situation where you are walking through a fairly rough neighbourhood and you see a gang of young men congregated on the pavement ahead of you. If you are streetwise and aware, the warning lights may begin to flash. Do you feel safe about walking right through the gang, or would you feel more comfortable crossing the road?

If you feel nervous in any way, then act on your instincts and cross over. It may seem an absurd precaution when nothing has actually happened, but it's far more absurd to ignore your gut reaction and walk straight into a nasty scene.

Sally found herself confronted by just such a choice. Six youths were hanging around her street corner as she was returning from work. She was dressed smartly and weighed down with bags of shopping. Her heart began to race, and she just knew it would be foolish to carry on past the youths, especially as there was nobody else in sight. She went into a nearby shop and waited a few minutes. When she came out, they were still there, but some other people had now appeared, so she judged it a little safer to continue home. Still nervous, she took the precaution of crossing the road and adjusted her handbag so it was tucked under her arm. Her housekeys she had transferred to a pocket. She walked purposefully and tried to appear both alert and relaxed at the same time.

What happened next she's never forgotten: she heard running feet and then saw the gang bearing down on a man on their side of the road. They beat him over the head, snatched his briefcase and wallet, and were away in seconds.

She says she'll never know for sure why they went for him rather than her, but she has no doubt that by listening to her instincts and acting on her fear, she reduced the likelihood of becoming the victim. Nor can she say precisely why she felt bad about those youths except that they conformed to her stereotyped image of young thugs. We all have those images and we should use them.

The anecdote illustrates another important point: surprise is the attacker's trump card, but it's one that we can also make our own. In Sally's case, she had registered and made it plain (by crossing the road) that she had seen the gang and perceived a threat. *She* had surprised *them* by taking positive steps to avoid them, and she therefore no longer conformed to their image of the unsuspecting victim.

What signals does your body give your?

In any situation like Sally's it's alertness to the early warning signals that can make the difference between safety and danger. Don't ignore those signals or write them off as 'silly'. They rarely are.

The signs of fear are unequivocal:

* Your stomach starts to churn.
* You may start to sweat although you actually feel cold.
* Your heart races.
* You find you're holding your breath.
* Your eyes and your ears strain.
* You feel wide awake, poised for action.

Listen for the signals, read them and ACT.

What sort of action is appropriate?

Once more, it should be stressed that no two situations and no two attackers will be the same, and the best any one of us can ever do is give plenty of advance thought to how we might react under attack. Chapter 6 looks more closely at appropriate responses if you are attacked. For the purposes of this chapter, it's useful to examine how you would react to a variety of hypothetical attacks. What, for example, would you do in the following circumstances?

Situation 1: You are out for a walk, and you become aware of being followed by a man on foot.
Situation 2: A man is following you in a car.
Situation 3: Somebody snatches your bag.
Situation 4: A man comes up behind you and touches your breasts or your bottom.

Situation 5: You receive a series of obscene phone calls.

Let's examine each in turn.

Situation 1

Here you should try and confirm first of all that you are being followed: cross the road, and keep recrossing it if you have to. A lot of 'followers' will be embarrassed by your obvious awareness of their presence, and will drop away. Others may not, and in this case you have a series of options. The best, to my mind, is to head for a public place where there are plenty of other people, or to go into a shop, pub or whatever. An alternative is to hammer on somebody's front door. If you're in a quiet residential area, this may be your best option: be prepared to hammer on as many doors as you have to. Don't lead the man back to your home, unless you know you have friends or family waiting for you there and there is nowhere else for you to get help.

A more assertive approach is to turn round and tell the man to go away.

This tactic was adopted by Kate, who discovered she was being followed when returning home late one night. She walked briskly towards her flat, hoping she could get in before the man reached her. Just as she reached the front door, he pounced, whereupon she swung round and bellowed: 'Get lost you, f***ing pervert!' He was evidently so surprised that he did just that.

Kate tells me that she has no idea where she got the courage from, but she recalls that her action was prompted by sheer fury and indignation. The tale certainly backs up the widely accepted theory that attackers rely on a passive reaction from women. When a target responds aggressively they pull back. You're surprising him, rather than letting him surprise you.

To recap, then, if you are being followed, the following responses are appropriate:

● Cross the road and try to shake him off this way.

- If this fails, make for a public place and get help.
- Do not lead him down a dead-end road where you can be trapped.
- Hammer on a front door – preferably one where you know the occupants.
- Alternatively, turn round and tell the man to go away. Don't worry if he denies he was following you – he would, wouldn't he?

Situation 2

If the man's following you in a car, the same principles apply, with a few additional points:

- Walk facing oncoming traffic, so that it's harder for someone to pull up behind you.
- If a man does draw up and ask the way, keep a good distance between yourself and the car – he's probably totally harmless, but if he isn't, he may try and drag you into the car with him.
- If a car does stop and you are threatened, don't hang around: bellow loudly, draw as much attention to yourself as you can and run in the opposite direction.

Situation 3

When someone grabs your bag, the first rule is to let it go.

Nicky lost her bag this way in Barcelona, and immediately took off in pursuit of the thieves – the bag contained many treasured possessions. Fortunately she was stopped by passers-by who told her the men most probably carried knives and that a handbag wasn't worth getting stabbed for. They were right, of course. I doubt if any preparation could have stopped that theft, which occurred in a busy street while it was still light. But had Nicky thought through the situation in advance she could have minimised the grief and inconvenience: she could have duplicated her diary and address book (both of which were lost) and she could have left at the hotel all the precious inessentials. Had she been at home in

England, she might have lost her flatkeys. At the time, she made a mental note for the future to carry them, plus some cash, in her pocket.

A friend of mine did, in fact, hang on to her camera when a man on a scooter tried to grab it from her in Rome. She spun around and managed to keep hold of the camera – but at a price. She sprained her ankle and hobbled in pain for several weeks. The camera was insured, and I think she wondered why she'd fought so hard for it.

The basic steps, then, if someone grabs for your bag or similar are as follows:

- Wear the strap over your head and across your body, and keep a hand on the bag at all times.
- Carry only the essentials, so that the loss is minimal.
- Transfer cash and keys to a pocket.
- Duplicate diaries and address books.
- Let go of the bag rather than get involved in a fight for it.

Situation 4

What would you do if you were touched up? Lucy has a heartening tale of her reaction to this fourth situation.

She was travelling up an escalator in the Paris metro. There was nobody about other than the man standing directly behind her who suddenly put his hand up her skirt. For a confused second, she assumed the hand belonged to a friend playing a practical joke, but as she swung round, she saw this was not so. 'I didn't make a conscious decision,' she says, 'but I was furious, and I slapped the man hard on the face as I turned.' He looked surprised, then angry and then he spat at her. She took off at high speed and says she collapsed into hysterical laughter once she was outside. She then went off and spent a lot of money – this was apparently highly therapeutic! Afterwards she wondered at the wisdom of her action, and imagined what might have ensued had the man reacted. But the point is, that he didn't: like so many aggressors, he gave up once he realised this woman was going to put up a fight.

No one has the right to touch you uninvited, and women should make their anger known when molested by a stranger – Lucy couldn't have responded better. Try to overcome your embarrassment and disbelief ('It can't be happening') and react as follows if someone touches you up:

- If you're in a crowded public place, shame him by identifying him and telling the world what he has just done.
- If you can't bring yourself to do this, grind a high heel into his foot – it should cool his ardour.
- Shout at him, show him your fury – in most cases this will terrify him, as it's not the way he expects you to react.

Situation 5

Obscene phone calls are another form of aggression visited upon women by men. They can be distressing and very frightening. How best to react to them?

Whatever you do, *don't engage the caller in conversation and don't show him that he bothers you*. That's what gives him his thrill. There are many effective strategies for dealing with these pests. I list below the ones that I think work best:

- Hang up immediately, and in most cases he'll get bored and find someone else to bother.
- If that one fails, call out to a man (imagined or real) 'Hey Jack, this weirdo's on the line again. Can you come and talk to him?' The caller will have gone by the time you return to him.
- Alternatively, you could keep a whistle by the phone and blow it vigorously into the mouthpiece. He won't call back.
- If he does persist, however, you may have to change your phone number. It's a nuisance, but if you want some peace it's probably worth doing.

The above illustrations only show some of the ways we can deal assertively and effectively with situations that bother us. Later in this book I will deal more fully with specific ways of responding to attack. What I've tried to demonstrate here is that *we are not powerless*, and that although we can never anticipate the precise nature of an attack or an attacker, we can help ourselves by talking to other women about their experiences, and thinking through in advance the ways in which we might react – *positively*.

Arming yourself

Part of this process is thinking of ways in which you might arm yourself. The law states that it is illegal to carry anything specifically intended for use as a weapon. If you are attacked and you retaliate by stabbing the aggressor with a steel comb filed to a point, you could find that it is you who are deemed the offender. Clearly this is most unfair, but if you think about it, the law is really there to defend us from weapon-touting louts. Few of us would wish for the more liberal gun laws, for instance, of the United States.

There are, however, many 'weapons' a woman and her children can carry quite legally. If she is attacked, spraying her assailant in the face with hair lacquer could give her those vital seconds she needs to escape. You carry your 'weapons' not so that you can get into a prolonged fight with the guy – the chances are you'll come out the loser. All you want to do is inflict enough discomfort so that he's distracted. Then you run. 'Bash and dash' is how the tactic is often referred to.

Below are some of the best ways in which you can arm yourself:

- Hairspray, spray perfume and other aerosol-type products. Use these to blind an aggressor temporarily.
- A personal alarm. There are several on the market, but the best are those that lock and continue to function if you drop or throw them to one side. Alarms are available from

DIY stores and your local crime prevention officer, as well as many stationers.
- A bunch of keys. Hold these in your hand, with the keys spread between your fingers. If you have to punch your aggressor, he'll feel it.
- An umbrella or walking stick.
- A pen or a hat pin to jab at the attacker.

In every case, any of these implements will only be useful if you have them at hand. Make a habit of taking your alarm and your keys out of your handbag and having them at the ready.

Learning how to bellow

Your best weapon in most unpleasant situations will be your voice. Unfortunately, it's also liable to desert you in the heat of an attack. Countless women have reported that they went into 'freeze' when assaulted, and were quite unable to scream.

Maybe we'd be better at it if we practised using our voices LOUDLY – from time to time. If you're worried about disturbing your family or your neighbours, you can always muffle the sound with a pillow! Try roaring and bellowing, rather than producing a high-pitched shriek. The more aggressive and the less 'feminine' the noise, the greater its effectiveness. As I have already said, the vast majority of criminals are opportunists, not psychopaths, and they rely on their victim's acquiescence – they expect you to behave in the way female victims behave in the movies. The minute you overturn their perceptions, you wrong-foot them. Being cowardly, most of them will therefore turn and run as soon as you show strong (and surprising!) signs of resistance – and making a hullabaloo falls into that category. Encourage your children from an early age to holler if they're in danger.

Your appearance

Dress is one of the most hotly-contested subjects in the self-protection debate. Should we take the line of least resistance and cover ourselves up so that no one can accuse us (however wrongly) of 'asking for it'? Or should we make a stand, wear whatever we feel like wearing because it's our absolute right to do so?

My view is that while all women should be free to dress as we wish, it remains an inescapable fact that we are making ourselves more vulnerable if we do not take a few sensible steps. It is unfair that we should have to adapt our behaviour on account of a few offensive or aggressive men, but if our priority is to look after ourselves, we have no other option.

The measures I would recommend are as follows:

- Change into comfortable shoes you can run in if you have to walk home late.
- If you are wearing a short skirt or low-cut top, take a long coat with you – especially if you're using public transport or walking. You'll feel more comfortable and much safer – who wants to be leered at by drunks on the bus home?
- Cover up or remove any expensive jewellery.
- Remove dark glasses if they hamper your vision.
- Remove your Walkman so that you can hear.
- Tuck away long hair. Not only does it attract attention, it can also be grabbed by someone approaching you from behind.
- Try to keep cumbersome shopping, etc. to an absolute minimum.

None of these precautions limits your freedom to look as you please, and they all make good sense.

Long-term action

Being streetwise isn't just a matter of looking after yourself in situations where there's potential for danger. It's also about lobbying for change and working with other people to make society a safer place for us all.

Neighbourhood Watch schemes are one very effective way of getting involved. Launched only eight years ago, the national network of local schemes now covers one household in six, and is recognised as a powerful weapon against crime. More details about Neighbourhood Watch are supplied in Chapter 3.

There may be other specific shortcomings in your local services which you believe should be tackled – inadequate bus routes, policing, street lighting and so on. Approach your council, your MP and anybody else who can effect the necessary changes. If they don't respond, put pressure on them by involving the local radio station or newspapers. As individuals, we may feel voiceless, but acting together in groups as voters and taxpayers we can become powerful instruments for change.

Summary

This chapter has looked at the specific dangers that face women when they are out and about on foot, as well as examining the more general 'streetwise' philosophy which applies in any threatening situation. The principal points can be summed up as follows:

- It is up to YOU to look after yourself – don't depend on others.

- Learn to be aware of potential danger and listen to your intuition.

- Learn and respond to the signs of fear.

- Walk away from a situation if your gut feeling tells you it's dangerous.

- Learn to visualise and prepare yourself for potentially dangerous situations *in advance*.

- Adopt a set of practical precautions, and employ them *consistently* – e.g., always carrying your keys in your pocket and keeping a hand pressed against your bag.

- Arm yourself with legal weapons – they'll give you confidence.

- Learn how to shout rather than scream.

- Surprise and wrong-foot a potential attacker by reacting in a way he does not anticipate – e.g., shouting loudly, publicly humiliating him, showing your outrage.

- If you are out late and on your own, think about what you're wearing and make yourself less vulnerable.

- Get involved in long-term projects to improve your area . . . and finally . . .

- *Always believe that you are equal to your attacker and that you have every chance of beating him.*

CHAPTER 3

As Safe as Houses

Although the word 'home' conjures up images of safety and security, reality is often something quite different. While we're away, our homes can be entered, turned upside down and stripped of all valuables by complete strangers; and many burglaries actually take place while the victims are in the house.

Of greater concern is the fact that many assaults also take place in the victim's house or flat. According to a 1989 Home Office report on rape, we are indeed more likely to be attacked indoors than out. While these figures include attacks on women by intimates and relatives – an area which this book is not intended to cover – as well as attacks in places other than the home, such as the office, attacks by unknown intruders in the victim's house or flat do form a significant part of the picture.

In recognition of this, the Home Office report notes that there is 'some crime prevention potential in relation to rapes by strangers indoors'. It continues: 'Action taken to secure homes from burglary, and commonsense routines followed to prevent the entry to the home of unexpected callers, can also serve to reduce the possibility of rape.'

It is one of those peculiar facts of life that while we are usually careful to protect our property, we are frequently slapdash in our measures to protect ourselves. When we go away from home, we lock doors, set alarms and arrange for neighbours to collect the post. *But what about when we are inside the house?* How many of us have gone upstairs or out into the garden during a day at home, leaving back doors, windows and so forth wide open? Sadly, the days are gone when we could afford to be so lackadaisical, when unknown visitors could be welcomed in for a cup of tea. It is sad that we can no longer be as open as in the past, but if we are to protect ourselves and our families we have to recognise the dangers and then act.

The greater part of this chapter deals with the security options available and considers how we can make ourselves, our families and our belongings safer at home. The final section examines appropriate responses to disturbing situations that might arise at home.

Living alone

Dramatic changes in social attitudes and opportunities for women have meant that more and more of us are living alone – through choice, circumstance or a combination of the two. For the single, independent career woman, this is a positive and exciting development. But for many women – especially the elderly and infirm, and those who are coping on their own with young children – living alone can be a frightening reality. Even those of us who are young and strong, and who espouse feminist beliefs, have to admit that when things go bump in the night, it's comforting to know you have a man in the house. Inevitably, a lone woman is seen by the criminal as a soft target.

The good news is that *none of us have to be soft targets*. By adopting an assertive and determined attitude to attack we can often frighten the criminal away, whatever our physical limitations. Just think about all those heartening tales of 'frail' pensioners who have beaten off attackers, and you'll see what I mean.

Beyond that, however, we also have the power to reduce the chances of attack at home in the first place – and that must be our first priority. As in Chapter 2, we have to use our fear positively, examining it and transforming it into positive action. What sort of steps can each of us take? The basic precautions listed below are a good starting-point.

● Don't let your doorbell advertise to passers-by that you are female and on your own.

- Likewise, don't let the phone directory give away your sex or marital status – in the UK this should not be a problem, as BT's policy is to encourage women against this.
- Never label your housekeys with your name and address – if you lose them, you could be in trouble.
- Labels on holiday luggage should only bear your initials and no title.
- Consider your security arrangements. Are they adequate? If not, be prepared to spend time and money on the measures suggested in this chapter.

Outdoor lighting

Many of us feel at our most vulnerable as we are approaching and entering our homes at night, and not until we have closed the door behind us do we feel the tension ebb away. Each of us has her own set of fears, depending on where we live.

- If you live in a house, you may be especially worried about the shadows cast by trees and bushes around your front door – this can be especially frightening if you're in the country and miles from any neighbours.
- If you live in a block of flats, you may be anxious about the lack of lighting around the main entrance.
- If you live on a council estate, you may have to negotiate ill-lit walkways late at night.

For some women, those few dark yards that separate the front door from so-called civilisation are so terrifying that they refuse to leave their homes after nightfall. Good outdoor lighting can go a long way to changing all that, and it's an absolute priority wherever you live. Although your home may be ablaze with light inside, there is no knowing who could be hiding in the shadows beyond the door. Some basic outdoor lights can be a real deterrent against crime as well as an antidote to your fear, and the costs need not be exorbitant – all-night lighting can add as little as £4 to your annual electricity bill.

The front door

The most important position for a light is likely to be over your front door. For this to be effective when you return home late, you will need to plug it into a *timer switch*. Alternatively, you can buy a *light-sensitive timer* which flicks on the lights as dusk falls, or a device which detects body heat or movement, thereby activating the lights as you approach (this method is inappropriate if you live close to the road or have pets – passing traffic and animals can activate the lights). Choose the device that best suits your circumstances. Having a light over your front door will not only make you feel safer when you come home, it also helps you identify callers who appear unexpectedly after dark.

Pathways

If there is a pathway from your gate to the door, is it one that makes you nervous? If so, what can you do to improve matters? A short path can usually be covered by lights mounted on the house, but if your path is longer, you may need to install lights along the way. These should be mounted on poles, either short (if you want them to remain hidden by day) or tall, and can be wired up to a timer or a light-sensitive device. Again, the cost need not be prohibitive. And you may feel that if you can improve the quality of your life, the money will be well spent. If the pathway is concealed by shrubbery, you should consider cutting it back. The police recommend that bushes are trimmed to four feet high and that tree branches be pruned for the first eight feet from the ground.

Garages and outhouses

Garages and outhouses are also potential hazards, offering shadows and concealed corners where criminals – either real or imagined – can lurk. If you can afford an automatic garage door and lights, so much the better – you'll find the arrangement immensely reassuring when you do drive home at night. A programmable or sensor light unit as described above is a good alternative, enabling you to look about you from the safety of your car, before you get out to open the garage. Again, you must balance cost against the degree of anxiety you experience when you come home after dark.

Common areas in flats

Blocks of flats can pose other problems, not least of these being the question of who is responsible for providing outdoor lighting. If the property is privately owned, your best solution could be to contact the other residents and get them to club together for new lights. You are likely to discover that your worries will be echoed by many of your neighbours, who simply haven't got round to acting on their fear. In any event, you should contact your local crime prevention officer at the police station before you approach your neighbours. He can assess your requirements and advise you on likely costs, thereby providing you with a case when you do speak to the other residents. It may be that one or two refuse to chip in, and there's precious little you can do about that. If you feel the lighting (or any other security measure) is important, go ahead with it anyway. It's galling to subsidise those who refuse to pay for services from which they'll benefit, but sometimes it's unavoidable.

Council property

If your home is council-owned, it is the council's responsibility to ensure you are safe. Some councils will act upon residents' complaints of inadequate lighting and other security matters, but in other cases you may have to lobby through a tenants' or a women's group. Be persistent and make a nuisance of yourself if you have to – involving a local newspaper or radio station is often a good ploy. Your local council housing department should provide you with a safety survey, on request, and you can back up your case with recommendations from the crime prevention officer at your local police station.

Checklist for security lighting:

As a summary, then, you should consider the following security lighting options:

Front doors
A good light will make you feel safer when you return home after dark. Have it wired up to either:

- a timer switch.
- a light-sensitive timer.
- a heat/movement-sensitive device.

Choose the method that best suits your circumstances.

Pathways
If yours makes you nervous, take the following steps:

- fix lights to the building or along the pathway.
- wire them up to a timer or light-sensitive device.
- cut back any bushes or shrubbery.

Garages and outhouses
Your best options are:

- automatic garage doors.
- lights wired up to timers or sensor units.

Common areas in flats
Lighting matters should be dealt with by:

- assessing your needs – your local crime prevention officer will help you.
- approaching your neighbours with practical suggestions and likely costs;
- being prepared to go ahead with improvements even when some people refuse to contribute.

Council properties
It's the council's responsibility to ensure you're safe. If you aren't, you should act:

- lobby through local groups – be persistent.
- use the local newspaper or radio if necessary.
- get the support of your crime prevention officer.

For information on security lighting, contact your local electricity board (numbers can be found in the Yellow Pages). Other useful contacts include The Women's Design Service, who have published a report on safety for women in housing estates, and Matrix, a feminist architectural co-operative which carries out free work in the London area. Contact numbers for both these organizations are supplied on pages 137–8.

Securing common areas

Shared residency means that common areas *inside* blocks of flats and housing estates can also be nightmarish for women. Lack of adequate outdoor lighting is but one of the many terrors that can make homecoming a dash for the door through a no-man's (no-woman's?) land of dark stairs, hallways and corridors.

Start by identifying the problem areas in your building. Apart from inadequate outdoor lighting, as discussed above, what bothers you? The following checklist should help you identify where change is necessary:

- Are there too many unmanned entrances?
- Would you feel better if there were only one point of entry, manned 24 hours a day?
- Are the stairwells too dark?
- Is it the covered walkways that make you uncomfortable?
- Or are you anxious about the underground parking facilities?
- Are you concerned about the absence of an alarm in the lift?

Identify the problem first, and then act on it. If you need advice on measures appropriate to your building, call in the experts: your local crime prevention officer will be able to pinpoint all the vulnerable spots, and recommend appropriate measures, listing them in order of priority.

As with outdoor lighting, caring about your own security

may mean taking the initiative, and then consulting with your neighbours.

When Susan moved into her flat last year, she immediately noticed the inadequate lock on the front door. She contacted her local crime prevention officer who recommended a replacement, and then called in a locksmith for a quotation – at around £90 the job wasn't cheap, but she felt it was worth doing. She approached the two other residents in the building and, to her surprise and relief, discovered that they too had been unhappy with the old lock, but had never got round to changing it. They were delighted she was taking the initiative and happily paid their share of the costs. All of them sleep easier in their beds.

Individuals and tenants' groups across the country have successfully persuaded local authorities to improve security arrangements in council properties. Officials are coming to see the architectural shortcomings of buildings erected in previous decades, and they are being forced to make changes. Dangerous walkways were removed in a notorious London estate after complaints from residents, and crime has dropped dramatically. Elsewhere, a manned reception area with a controlled front entrance has replaced a system of several unlocked doors. Everyone feels very much safer. Once more, if you are afraid, try and work out how you could improve your environment. If you are unsure about what steps should be taken in your building, contact your crime prevention officer or one of the agencies recommended on page 137–8.

Securing your own home

Nobody wants to turn their house or flat into Fort Knox. If nothing else, the cost of adopting every security measure available is prohibitive. There is also an argument that if you deck your home with alarms, bars and fancy locks, you are actually advertising the high value of your possessions. Put it this way, if you are the only house in the street displaying an alarm box, you are all but saying that yours is the only property worth breaking in to. What we must all try to achieve is a level of security that doesn't draw attention to us, that we can afford and that makes us feel safe.

As with outdoor lighting and security measures for common parts, your best bet is to get expert advice before you act. If you are going to spend money, you might as well spend it on devices that work. The importance of this struck me when burglars broke in to my last flat: money had been spent on three sturdy front-door locks and a chain, but none of us had noticed the inadequacy of the door itself, which the criminals were able to kick through with ease. Afterwards, our crime prevention officer advised us to fit a stronger door and to reinforce the frame with a steel bar. Two locks would then suffice.

Wherever you live, and whatever your security needs, you should consider where your home is most easily penetrated by unwelcome visitors. The most vulnerable points in a property are:

- the front door
- the back or side door
- the patio door
- the windows.

Let's consider each of these in turn.

The front door

This should be made of solid wood, possibly with a steel bar reinforcing the lock side of the frame. You can give extra strength to the hinges by fitting security hinge bolts, which are not expensive, but if your door is firmly fixed with three 6-inch hinges, you're unlikely to need the hinge bolts.

Two locks are adequate. The first should be a mortice deadlock which can only be opened with a key, and which conforms at least to British Standard 3621. There are many different products on the market which would be appropriate, and prices start at about £20. Complement this with a rim lock which automatically deadlatches when you close the door. This prevents criminals from gaining access by sliding a knife or credit card between the door and frame. Again, the rim lock should conform to British Standard 3621. Prices range between about £25 and £60 at the time of writing.

It's imperative that once you've fitted these locks, you should use them – consistently. Reputable locksmiths will give you advice on appropriate locks for your home and your budget. It goes without saying, that a first priority when you move house or flat is to change the locks – you never know who else might have the keys to your home.

A chain is a useful device, so long as it's strong and well-fitted. Alternatively, you can buy a restraint deadlock (e.g., Yale 83), which automatically prevents the door from being opened more than about three inches. Elderly people living on their own should find one of these devices particularly reassuring should they have to answer the door to unexpected visitors. The same can be said for a door viewer, which allows you to look at the caller before you open the door. Don't open it if they arouse your suspicion. Tell your children they should *never* open the door to a stranger.

If you live in a block of flats, securing the door to your own flat is just as important as securing the main street entrance. All the precautions described above apply, with the important addition of a door telephone entry system. If you don't have one, raise the matter with your landlord and/or the other tenants. If you're a council tenant, you should speak with your local housing officials. Once the system is installed, be sure it's used properly.

Identify callers *before* you let them into the building, and don't let in people on behalf of absent neighbours.

The back or side door

This can be especially vulnerable as it is often concealed, and intruders can spend time working on the door with reduced risk of being spotted. Once more, the door should be of solid wood, with bolts fitted at the top and bottom, and with a mortice deadlock. If you want a glass panel fitted, to let in extra daylight, be sure it's of the reinforced variety, so that it cannot be smashed. Fit a chain if visitors are likely to call at this door.

The patio door

Generally these will be of the sliding variety, and should be fitted – top and bottom – with a key-operated lock bolt, such as the Ingersoll bolt for patio windows. Patio doors should also be fitted with a mortice lock, and an anti-lift device which stops a criminal from lifting the door off its rail. If you are ordering new patio doors, do check the locking arrangements and seek specialised advice before placing your order.

Windows

Windows are notorious, providing access for more than half of household intruders. While we may attend to doors, we are often careless about closing windows and fitting them with adequate locks. Even tiny windows can be penetrated – if the intruder can fit his head through the gap, he's able to squeeze the rest of his body through, too. With locks, he's forced to smash the glass first, and if you're in the house, you'll hear him coming. If you're not, there's a good chance someone else will, and in any case the criminal will be forced to think twice about breaking in.

Basement-level windows are the most vulnerable and it may be worth considering laminated glass (which is tougher to smash) or security grilles for extra protection – such measures could be a wise and comforting investment if you are, for instance, living alone in a basement flat. In any case, you should certainly install security locks on basement, ground floor and any other windows that are accessible (via flat roofs, balconies, porches, drainpipes, high walls, etc.). Windows that cannot be seen from the street should also be considered a priority.

Key-operated window locks are available from about £3 at DIY stores, and they're easily fitted. You should always keep keys near the window in case of fire – but obviously far enough away from unwelcome hands.

A final point about windows is that *people can see you through them*. Women living on their own are especially advised to have some sort of net curtaining and, at the very least, to ensure they do not undress without shutting out potential Peeping Toms.

Checklist for securing your home:

The main points outlined above can be summarised as follows:

- Seek expert advice before you act.
- Secure the most vulnerable points first (i.e. doors and windows).

The front door

- Have a good quality door.
- Ensure the hinges are strong.
- Fit two locks: a mortice deadlock and a rim lock – **use them**.
- Fit a chain or door restraint, plus a viewer.
- If you live in a block of flats, have a telephone entry system fitted on the street door.

The back/side door

- Have a good quality door.
- Fit bolts at top and bottom and a mortice deadlock.
- Any glass should be reinforced.
- Consider fitting a chain.

Patio doors

- Fit a key-operated locking bolt and a mortice lock.
- Fit an anti-lift device.
- Seek specialist advice if in any doubt.

Windows

- Fit good locks on any accessible windows – especially important if you're in a basement flat and on your own.
- Consider laminated glass or security grilles if you live on the ground floor/basement, and/or if you're alone.
- Be aware of the possibility of Peeping Toms – keep curtains drawn at night (especially if you live alone) and consider hanging net curtains.

A note on alarms

Home security can be a costly business, and most people should concentrate their resources on fitting solid doors and sturdy locks, as recommended above. In the majority of cases these measures will suffice to deter criminals, and they should be your first priority. If you opt for an alarm system as well, don't fall into the common trap of choosing one so sophisticated that you're afraid to use it. Be sure to choose one that's simple, practical and which suits your lifestyle.

Dealing with specific situations

So far this chapter has dealt entirely with practical security measures for the home, all of which are a vital part of any self-protection programme. In most instances, they will reduce both our fear and the likelihood of burglary and attack.

In some situations, however, we may need more than the above-mentioned security measures if we are to ensure our safety.

What, for instance, do we do if a stranger does come to the door? If a plumber becomes amorous? If we wake up to find an intruder in the house?

It's important that each of us gives advance thought to how we would cope in any of these situations.

The examples below illustrate an appropriate pattern of behaviour:

The bogus official

Con men appear on our doorsteps in many imaginative guises – they may pretend they're gasmen, electricians, salesmen, preachers, officials from the local authority, window cleaners or anybody else. But what they really are is a group of sick individuals with a propensity to prey upon the elderly and the lonely who are only too pleased to invite them in for a cup of tea and a chat. Some of the most cruel and professional confidence tricks are carried out by children on old people. Be on your guard against anyone.

- Fitting a chain and spyhole to your door will enable you to take a look at the stranger without letting him into your house.
- If he says he wants to sell you something, a simple 'No thank you' is all that's required from you. Don't be afraid to say it.
- If he claims he's from the gas board or some other official body, ask him to show you his card.
- If you are still anxious, ask him to wait while you phone his office to check he is bona fide – *the number on his card may be fake, so look up his employers in the phone book.*
- If he objects, or if you have any other reason to suspect his motives, call the police immediately.
- If you have children, tell them they should never let a stranger into the house – especially when you are out.

Don't be afraid of appearing silly or rude. If the man is genuine, he should be happy to wait until you feel secure.

The amorous plumber
Sometimes bona fide visitors to your home can turn nasty. Even mild sexual remarks can be alarming for a woman on her own, and we all need to know how to deal with the situation.

Astonishing though it may sound, many unwanted suitors claim they have picked up inviting signals from the woman. Although in a lot of cases this is merely an excuse for inexcusable behaviour, one can also infer that some men truly are vain and stupid enough to read messages where there are none. In an ideal world, it is they who should be educated, they who should learn that when a woman says 'No', she means it. But ours isn't an ideal world, and if we're to protect ourselves, we have to make very sure there is nothing in our behaviour that can be misconstrued.

- By all means be pleasant to any genuine visitor you let into your house, but *maintain a professional distance.*
- Make him tea or coffee, but don't stand around chatting to him.

- And remember, although he may be from your local plumbing firm, and therefore 'trustworthy', he is also a stranger and an unknown quantity – so don't open the door to him in your dressing gown.
- Always try to keep your paths of flight clear – if he makes a lunge for you, you want to be able to escape.

Usually there will be signals in advance of any unwelcome attention. There will be flattering comments, remarks – perhaps – about how lonely you must get on your own, questions about your love life and confidences about his. Often this banter is harmless, if irritating, but sometimes it's a prelude to an unwelcome sexual advance. Joining in with and encouraging the chat may be construed by the man as an invitation for more. *Don't give him the opportunity to do so.*

If you do begin to feel threatened, act on your instincts before anything happens:

- Leave the house – tell him you're going shopping if that makes you feel better.
- Call a friend.
- Say your husband/boyfriend or any other male is due back shortly.

Don't be afraid of appearing rude – it's not in your interests to be polite.

The night-time intruder

It's our worst fear, and the one that we do the least to conquer. How often have you lain awake at night, listening to imagined intruders, only to discover that it's the central heating up to its tricks once more?

We can do a lot to eliminate this unnecessary terror, by adopting the security measures described in the early part of this chapter. The vast majority of intruders will only break in where it's easy for them to do so.

We can also help ourselves by learning the natural sounds of our own home. Listen to the creaks and get to know the strange noises your home emits during the night. You'll sleep better and you'll also be better prepared should an intruder break in.

If the worst does happen, and you wake to hear someone in your house:

- Get up and make some noise.
- Call out to an imaginary imaginary male partner if you're alone.
- Whatever you do, *don't confront the burglar.*

In the vast majority of cases he will make a swift exit when he hears you moving about. He doesn't want trouble – he's at least as afraid as you are.

Install a phone beside your bed, so that you can call the police immediately, and if you have a burglar alarm, have an emergency button fitted by your bed.

A community spirit

My local crime prevention officer told me that by far the most common mistake he encounters is people's failure to familiarise themselves with their surroundings. More than anything else, he recommends that we get to know our neighbourhood and our neighbours, and actively look out for the welfare of one another. Keep an eye on one another, exchange phone numbers and be prepared to act if you see any activity around a neighbour's home which arouses your suspicion – you'd want them to do the same for you, wouldn't you?

These days we are predisposed to minding our own business, to walking by when we see someone in trouble. This has to change if we're to make our communities safer places in which to live. Isn't it better to seem a little nosy than to ignore the noises of a break-in next door?

Neighbourhood Watch schemes are one of the most effective ways in which ordinary people can help deter crime in their area. Originally established in 1962, the national network now numbers some 60,000 schemes.

If your area is not covered, and you're interested in setting up a scheme, you should take the following steps:

- Contact your local police for advice, guidance and support.
- Find out if your neighbours are interested in the idea.
- Appoint a co-ordinator, who will act as the link between your group and the police, and who will also administer the scheme.
- Arrange a first meeting and invite everyone in your area to attend. The police will explain how the scheme works.
- Once the scheme is up and running, maintain an active interest in it – that's the only way you'll achieve long-term results.

'Make a success of Neighbourhood Watch' is a useful twenty-minute video, designed to guide anyone interested in setting up a scheme. Details of how to obtain a copy are supplied on page 135.

Summary

This chapter has considered ways of preventing burglary and assault at home. It has also provided examples of how you might deal with an intruder or attacker. The principal points are summarised below:

- If you live alone, don't advertise the fact that you do.

- Look at your outdoor lighting arrangements. If they're inadequate, invest some time and money in improving them – front doors, pathways and garages/outhouses are the danger zones.

- Cut back bushes and shrubbery around your front door.

- In blocks of flats, be prepared to take responsibility for and act upon inadequate security measures in common areas – bully the council if you're a council tenant.

- Secure the vulnerable points in your own home, paying special attention to doors and windows. Seek expert advice if you have any doubts about what you should do – crime prevention officers and locksmiths are the best sources of information.

- In blocks of flats, have a telephone entry system installed.

- Consider installing an alarm – but make sure it's one you know how to use!

- Be suspicious about any stranger who arrives on your doorstep – don't be afraid of appearing rude.

- Teach your children never to let strangers into the house, however friendly they might seem.

- Beware of amorous plumbers – keep a professional distance at all times, and keep your paths of flight clear.

- If you wake up to the sounds of a nocturnal intruder, get up and make a noise. *Don't* confront him.

- Install a phone by your bed, so that you can call the police immediately.

- Get to know your neighbours and your neighbourhood. Join or set up a Neighbourhood Watch scheme.

CHAPTER 4

Safety at Work

How great is the threat at work?

It may come as a surprise to many women to learn that we are less likely than our male colleagues to suffer violent attack at work. According to research comissioned by the Suzy Lamplugh Trust in March 1989, an average of one in ten men suffers physical aggression at work, a figure which rises to one in three for male professionals whose jobs take them away from their workplace. For women, the likelihood of violent attack is one in fourteen. These statistics are heartening for us, painting as they do a reality that is rarely admitted by a male-dominated society: men are victims too.

Notwithstanding, women *do* have to deal with the threat of violence at work, as well as a range of other forms of intimidation which may not result in physical injury, but which can be chronically damaging to our welfare. I'm talking, of course, of sexual harassment which even in its mildest form constitutes an act of aggression, and therefore merits discussion in this book.

To give some perspective on what is now accepted as a mounting problem, the Trust's report revealed that one in seven of the respondents (male and female) had suffered some form of sexual harassment at work. The great majority of these cases were women. The incidents and their aftermaths were varied.

- One woman – a planner – suffered leering and wolf-whistling from male colleagues on a building site.

- Another was promised promotion in return for sex.
- Yet another woman was continually touched up and then assaulted by a 'superior'.

In every case, the victims suffered at the very least from anxiety, depression and a sense of deep degradation. Occasionally victims of this sort of outrage may be forced to suffer much more: rape, abduction and even murder of women who thought they were simply doing another day's work.

The workplace can and does expose us to unpleasantness and aggression which threaten our well-being, both physical and emotional. All of us need to examine our own situation, and ask ourselves a few questions.

- Do we live in apprehension or even fear of harassment and/or violence as a result of our job?
- If we do, is it really right that we should?
- Is our employer aware of our anxieties?
- How could the risks be removed?
- And what can we do to help ourselves?

Our attitude must be assertive (especially if our employers are resistant to change) and our aim must be to remove the cause of our anxiety before it hurts us or our colleagues.

Who is at risk?

The nature of our work determines the specific risks we face, and this is especially true where actual physical (as opposed to verbal) aggression is concerned. For instance, bank staff, and others who handle money, are unlikely to face the same problems as nurses, who may be dealing with the disturbed; they, in turn, don't face the problems of estate agents or journalists who may have to meet strangers outside the office. Sexual harassment is another matter: it's a problem we may all encounter, irrespective of what we do.

For most of us, the risk of attack is mercifully small. Those who fall into the higher risk category are likely to work in one of the following capacities:

- You work alone (e.g. salespeople).
- You work in a 'male' environment (e.g. the City).
- You have appointments outside your office (e.g. estate agents).
- You work 'on view' (e.g. estate agents, bank staff).
- You frequently work late or out of office hours (e.g. any professional).
- You handle cash (e.g. retail staff).
- You are providing care, advice or training (e.g. teachers and nurses).
- You enforce the law (e.g. debt collectors).
- You work with mentally disturbed or other potentially violent people (e.g. social workers).
- You work in an area hit by public expenditure cuts (e.g. benefit officers).

Women who do work under the above conditions frequently put themselves in situations they would never tolerate ordinarily, simply because they feel they 'have to' if they're going to keep their job. An architect may, for instance, have real fears about entering an empty site development on her own, but a greater fear of being seen as 'inferior' to her male colleagues may drive her into danger, despite her instincts. Or an estate agent may agree to meet an unknown male at an empty property, knowing that she would never put herself in a parallel situation outside work, but knowing too that she'll lose her job if she can't perform this fundamental function.

Do we really have take these risks?

Do we have to continue to run the gauntlet in our working lives?

Does somebody have to get hurt before our employers will sit up and take note?

Or is there something we can do NOW to reduce the risk and attendant stress?

Our employers' legal duty to protect us

Whether they like it or not, our employers have a duty to protect us from aggression suffered in the course of our work, and they are breaking the law if they ignore it. This duty is enshrined in Section 2(1) of the 1974 Health and Safety at Work Act which obliges them to take all 'reasonably practicable' steps to safeguard our safety and welfare. Such steps include protecting us from the risk of assault by people with whom we come into contact while doing our job.

Employers are therefore obliged to:

• Provide a safe working place.
• Provide safe systems of work.
• Identify the hazards presented by any particular job.
• Find measures to remove the hazards and reduce any risk.
• Provide information and training for staff.

Employers who resist taking steps to protect us should be reminded of their obligations under law. The qualifying phrase 'reasonably practicable' may be used as a let-out by unscrupulous employers. They may argue that the cost of introducing improvements outweighs the risk to employees. But in fact, for that argument to hold up in court, the risk would have to be so insignificant as to be virtually non-existent. And there is a further consideration for employers who are unwilling to comply with their obligations: any costs they incur will be offset by the savings from a reduction in violent incidents and/or sickness leave and claims for compensation. A happy staff, which feels it has the support of management, will be more productive and better for business.

The Sex Discrimination Act also lays obligations on management. Section 41(3) of the Act states that employers are liable for any discriminatory act committed by their employees in the course of their employment – which could include acts of sexual harassment committed by a male employee against a female.

If you feel your employer is acting irresponsibly you should seek advice from your union, if you have one, or from the

Health and Safety Executive – until very recently, the HSE was reluctant to tackle irresponsible employers, but it is now strong enough to take legal action on the behalf of staff.

Identifying the problems in your job

Not all employers wish to dodge their duties. A frequent reason for failure to protect staff is ignorance: management is not aware of a problem, and if it is, it does not know how or where to start tackling it. Identifying risks in our own job and seeking solutions must therefore be the responsibility of each one of us. If we are worried about our safety at work, then we should make it our own business to speak to colleagues and discover how widespread the problem is – irrespective of our employer's attitude.

If, for instance, a client is subjecting you to degrading sexual remarks, ask other women in the office if they've been pestered by the same man. Or, if you're anxious about the frequency with which you have to meet unknown clients outside the office and outside working hours, try and find out if others share your worries. Only by discovering the precise nature and extent of the problem can you begin to find an appropriate solution. In some situations (especially where you are dealing with disturbed and potentially violent clients), the men you work with are likely to be as concerned as the women. They'll be delighted someone has raised the issue. And rallying colleagues around you will not only give you a greater degree of confidence in dealing with your particular problem, it will also increase the likelihood of your employer taking the issue seriously.

Many of us believe we have no power to change our working conditions. But the fact is, we do.

Taking steps and devising a preventive strategy

In its booklet *Violence to Staff* the Health and Safety Executive recommends to employers a step-by-step approach to aggression in the workplace:

- Gather as much information as you can about the nature and scale of the problem, as described above.
- Once you have assessed the size of the problem and the level of stress it creates, institute a formal system for recording and classifying incidents. The idea is to encourage staff to come forward when they are anxious about any form of aggression or violence they encounter through work, and to *normalise* that act of coming forward.
- Next, appropriate preventive measures should be sought and put into practice.
- Finally, those measures should be monitored and continually reassessed, to ensure they have the desired effect and that vital lessons will be learned should incidents recur. If the harassment, aggression or risk of violence remains, there should be the flexibility to go back to the drawing-board and come up with new ideas.

Violence to Staff assumes close employer/employee co-operation in advising this process, and is therefore addressing the problem of workplace aggression in terms of an ideal world. Nevertheless, the basic principles – which are sound – can be applied to most situations, and provide a good working model for us to follow. The examples below, which look at the most common forms of aggression at work, illustrate how this practical process can be adapted to a variety of circumstances.

Sexual harassment in the office

The offender may be a colleague, possibly someone whom you liked and respected at one time, but who has now offended you by his behaviour. Or it may be someone whom you have never met, but with whom you do business down the telephone – his constant sexual remarks offend and irritate you.

Typical forms of sexual harassment include:

- Unnecessary touching.
- Suggestive remarks and verbal abuse – both face to face and over the phone.

- Comments (either flattering or insulting) about your clothes, your shape, your attractiveness.
- Whistling at you.
- Displaying pin-ups in the office where you both work.
- Reading pornographic material in your presence.
- Demanding sex from you.
- Assaulting you.

It is important to make a clear distinction between this type of one-sided behaviour and the reciprocal – and thus acceptable – flirtatious or romantic relationship that may develop between two people.

These problems can be particularly hard to deal with if you are young and inexperienced; and if you work as receptionist your constant contact with colleagues and strangers will mark you out as a highly vulnerable target. If you are having trouble and you aren't sure how to cope, why not contact your personnel manager? If that's not an option, seek out a sympathetic senior colleague and explain your worries. There are few women who would not act in your support.

Whatever your professional relationship with the man (he may be your boss, you may be his), he has no right to use you as a sexual object or offend you as a woman. Keeping your mouth shut, and hoping the problem will go away, seldom works and is frequently interpreted by the man as tacit encouragement. You must act fast to protect yourself from further unpleasantness.

Steps for stopping sexual harassment

- Your first move – the information-gathering stage – is to talk to female colleagues. Does this man habitually bother women? Has he been complained about in the past? Is the problem of sexual harassment rife in the office? The mere fact of sharing your worries will restore you, and you'll feel boosted by the support of others.
- Next, you should speak to the man. Ask him to stop behaving like this, and explain – if necessary – what it is

that offends you. You must be specific in what you say, so plan this conversation in advance. You may find it helpful to enlist the support of a friend, who could back you up and impede further harassment.

- Alternatively you could write to the man – you may find this easier and less embarrassing than confronting him.
- Finally, you might try giving him a taste of harassment: plaster his walls with male pin-ups, slap his bottom, get a gang of female colleagues to leer at him. Admittedly, such tactics are pretty low, but sometimes they're the only language a persistent pest will understand.

If he continues to trouble you, you will have to take further action. This could take the form of complaining to your superiors, contacting your union or – as a last resort – taking legal action. Whichever road you go down, you will need *evidence*. Keep a diary of the man's behaviour, and ask a friend to do likewise.

A booklet issued by Liberty (formerly the NCCL) – *Sexual Harassment at Work* – suggests that we use the Sex Discrimination Act to oblige employers to clamp down on harassment. As I wrote earlier in this chapter, the Act makes employers responsible for the discriminatory behaviour of their staff – which could include the acts of sexual harassment described above. The employer only escapes liability if he can prove he has taken 'reasonably practicable steps' to prevent the discrimination.

If you are being harassed at work by a colleague, you can use the Act to involve your employers. Employers who *are* concerned, and who wish to comply with their obligations can take a number of long-term initiatives:

- They can produce a written statement condemning sexual harassment.
- They can create formal channels of complaint.
- They can demonstrate a commitment to disciplinary action.
- They can set up a body to review all of these matters regularly.

If your company has already adopted such measures, use them.

Meeting clients on your own and away from the office

This is quite a different type of problem, and one which fewer of us will ever have to confront. The Suzy Lamplugh case, however, demonstrated to us all that its consequences can be devastating. Most women return safely from their appointments, but many have taken unacceptable risks to their personal safety in going: they have met a total stranger at an address they may not have been to before; nobody has been aware of their whereabouts or their expected time of return; nobody, other than the woman in question, has a record of the male client's identity – and that's written in the notebook she carries with her at all times.

The circumstances I've just described are perfectly run-of-the-mill if you're a journalist, an estate agent, a saleswoman, or anybody else whose work involves one-to-one meetings with strangers outside the office. The dangers are quite obvious when committed to paper like this, but they usually only surface when someone like Suzy Lamplugh goes missing.

Most jobs will not require drastic measures. Usually it will suffice to take a few simple precautions, and incorporate these into our daily working practices. They are as follows:

- Colleagues should inform one another of potentially difficult clients.
- You should leave behind in the office a diary which notes the client's name, where and when you are meeting, and an estimated time of return – if you are self-employed, leave these details with a friend or neighbour.
- Any new client should be checked up on – when he phones in to make the appointment, find out as much about him as you can, and then check that he's telling the truth.
- If you arrive at a meeting and feel anxious, ask to phone your office and leave a contact number.
- Liaise with a colleague when you go out: phone them when

you arrive and when you're on your way back, and prearrange a distress code which will not arouse suspicion – if self-employed, ask a friend to be your 'base'.

- Be prepared to leave a meeting if you really feel nervous – think of an excuse in advance.
- Get your employer to provide training and to produce a handbook describing these procedures.
- Ask your employer to issue mobile phones to field staff.

In the social services it's established practice for staff to double up when they are visiting a potentially violent client, and on the rare occasions where we know it's foolhardy to go alone we should explore this option with our employers. Many of us may have long wished to do so, but have never tried because we haven't wished to jeopardise our professional reputation. But if you think about it, how professional is it to walk into a situation that you instinctively know to be dangerous? If we can elicit the support of colleagues, who's to say management will not co-operate? If they refuse to, and you feel you have a genuine cause for concern, seek the support of your union or the Health and Safety Executive.

In the end, we all have to take responsibility for our own safety: if you feel the level of risk is intolerable, and your employer is not prepared to reduce that risk, you should consider leaving the job.

Working late in an empty office

Here is a situation with which many professional women will be familiar – lawyer friends of mine, in particular, are frequently required to work into the small hours to prepare cases for the following day, and some have spoken of the ease with which an intruder could get into their office. In many firms after-hours security arrangements adequately protect those who have to stay on late – there are systems to ensure all windows and doors are locked, and guards patrolling the building – but elsewhere, security is slapdash.

There are a number of practical steps you and your employer

can take if you are worried about being interrupted by an intruder:

- Locking outside doors and windows at the end of the day should be somebody's responsibility – leaving them open is a risk to security.
- Vetting of visitors at the reception area should be rigorous – no stranger should be allowed to wander in without thorough checking.
- If you're alone in the building, tell the security guard where you are, and ask him to drop in on you on his rounds; tell him you will check out with him when you leave.
- Phone a friend and tell them where you are – say you'll ring when you get home.
- If it's really late when you leave, get a taxi home or to the station – taxis will be discussed more fully in Chapter 5.

If you are still anxious at the prospect of working late in a deserted office, ask yourself if you really have to. Could you not come in early the next morning instead? Could you perhaps take the work home, or to a friend's home? Try and think round the problem, and don't ever accept fear as something you have to put up with.

Working with clients who may become violent

Those who provide a service to the public are most likely to encounter this type of aggression – sometimes on a daily basis. Benefit officers, retail workers, hospital employees and bank staff are all obvious examples of people whose work brings them into regular contact with frustrated, angry and potentially violent clients. But many other jobs put us at risk too. If you do encounter this problem in your work, you'll need to do something about it: find out if it's common in your field, what your employer is doing to protect you, and look for ways in which you can protect yourself.

The aggression can be triggered in many ways: having to wait for ages in unappealing surroundings; clients feeling they are the victims of unnecessary bureaucracy; staff dealing unsympathetically with those clients, and so forth. By first tackling these sources of grievance, we can do much to reduce the stress and so protect ourselves from violence. The best way of finding out where the problems in your workplace are, is by asking colleagues. These are the sort of questions you should be looking at:

- The environment: can waiting areas be made more congenial, with better furnishings, reading material, drinks machines, etc?
- Information systems: can these be improved, so that clients are not kept in the dark about length of waiting time, etc?
- Staff training: have staff been adequately trained to deal with difficult situations, and to handle clients sympathetically?

Practical security measures can also be taken, which will make you – the employee – feel much safer:

- Emergency communications could be installed – e.g. panic buttons.
- Videos and protective screens could be introduced, although it's also important to maintain a welcoming atmosphere.
- Personal alarms and/or portable phones could be issued to field staff.
- Interview rooms could be designed so that the interviewer is near the door and able to make a quick exit.

If someone does become violent, the following points should be born in mind:

- Do not attempt to control the situation single-handed unless you have no alternative.
- Walk away, if you can.
- Use physical restraint as a last resort.

81

On a more long-term basis, employers should think about the following issues:

- Are staffing levels adequate?
- Are employees adequately trained to deal with stressed clients? (Nervous/inexperienced staff can be as provocative as those who are offhand, authoritarian or bossy.)
- Is there a formal policy on reacting to danger and to alarm signals?
- Are all employees trained in this policy?
- Is there an efficient system whereby staff swap information on difficult clients?

A note on lifts

There can be few situations more alarming than that of being trapped in a lift with an assailant. But fortunately there are a number of things we can do to prevent this situation, and to defuse it should it arise.

- If it's just you and him waiting for the lift, and you feel uncomfortable – *don't get in*. Invent an excuse, if it makes you feel better ('Damn – I've forgotten my files'), and either take the next lift or use the stairs.
- If there's no one else in the building apart from this man, be even more cautious.
- If you do get in with a man or group of men, stand facing them (but avoiding eye contact) and next to the controls. Locate the alarm.
- If you are assaulted, press every button you can lay your hands on – including the alarm. Even if he has hold of your arms, you may be able to throw your weight against the control panel.
- Bellow as loudly as you can and show him your fury.
- If he persists, inflict some pain on him (see Appendix), press the controls and flee at the first opportunity.

A note about your possessions

It is easy to be casual about your possessions in an office where you know and trust all your colleagues. But think twice before leaving your handbag at your desk while you leave the room for a few minutes. *Are you sure you know everyone who comes into the building?* Err on the side of caution, and either keep your valuables with you at all times, or have them in a locked drawer.

Responsible employers will have set up sound security systems, with vetting procedures at reception. If you feel that you aren't adequately protected from strangers wandering in from the street, you should launch a campaign for change.

Taking a long-term view

There are, then, many ways in which we can act to counter the risk of aggression and/or violence at work. We're all capable of improving our working conditions, and we must learn to think positively about solutions to situations that worry us. Nobody should be expected to brave unnecessary danger in the course of their job.

Beyond the short-term solutions, there must be a long-term policy commitment by employers to look after their staff. Once the problem of aggression has been raised, management should introduce a formal complaints procedure and keep detailed records of further incidents – a systematic approach is absolutely essential if the risk of violence is to be reduced.

In a high-risk job, awareness training should be introduced for both male and female staff, and self-defence training should also be considered. Refresher courses are essential.

Management should also make it clear to staff that they will be supportive in the event of an attack, and have a defined plan of action at the ready – victims may be in need of leave, of counselling, compensation and legal advice, and it will help them if their employer acts swiftly and sympathetically on these requests.

Employers and employees seeking more information on how violence may be reduced in the workplace should buy a copy of the Health and Safety Executive's booklet *Preventing Violence to Staff*. The TUC and some individual trade unions have also published advice for specific types of job, and may be contacted for help and information. Local police crime prevention officers will recommend, on request, suitable measures to reduce the risk of violence in your job.

Summary

Many women face risks to their personal security through their work. In this chapter I have sought to identify those risks and suggest ways in which they might be reduced. The main points are listed below:

- Determine the nature of the risk you face in your job.

- Refuse to accept that you must put up with those risks in order to retain your job.

- Remind your employers of their responsibilities under law and seek the support of your trade union or the Health and Safety Executive if needs be.

- In any situation, devise a strategy for eliminating risk:
  - assess the nature and level of the problem;
  - institute a formal system for recording and classifying incidents;
  - seek and put into practice appropriate measures;
  - monitor and reassess the effectiveness of the measures.

- If you're being sexually harassed by a colleague, take action:
  - find out if anyone else is suffering too, and keep a diary of the man's behaviour – get a friend to do likewise;
  - tell the man that you will not tolerate his behaviour;
  - give him a taste of harassment if he persists;
  - remind your employers of their responsibilities under the Sex Discrimination Act.

- If you have to meet clients on your own and away from the office, make a habit of taking basic precautions:
  - colleagues should inform one another of troublemakers;
  - leave behind in your office details of the meeting;
  - run a thorough check on new clients;
  - if you're anxious in a meeting, phone your office;
  - prearrange a distress code with a colleague at your office;
  - leave if you feel really nervous;
  - ask your employer actively to support these measures and to issue mobile phones to field workers;
  - double up with a colleague where necessary;
  - consider resigning if the level of risk is unacceptable.

- If you have to work late in an empty office:
  - institute an office system for locking doors and windows;
  - ensure vetting of visitors is vigorous and consistent;
  - tell the security guard where you are;
  - tell a friend where you are, and phone them when you get home;
  - consider alternatives to working late if you're unhappy with the situation.

- If you have to work with potentially violent clients you should:
  - get your employer to tackle the source of frustration by improving the working environment, information systems and staff training;
  - improve practical security measures in your place of work;
  - encourage your employers to think about long-term measures and policies for dealing with violent clients.

- Don't travel alone in a lift with someone who makes you uncomfortable.
- Look after your possessions at all times, and encourage your employer to set up effective security measures.
- Lobby for a long-term policy commitment from your employer on aggression at work.

CHAPTER 5

Getting from A to B – Safely

The fear of travel

The greatest concern of many women is not the violence they may encounter at work, but the dangers of their journey there and back. As pressure mounts to work longer (and therefore later) hours, the problem of getting home unscathed increases.

Of course the problem isn't confined to those with jobs. All of us have to travel, many relying on a public transport system that seems to have little regard for our safety. Indeed, our wariness of trains and buses means that as many as half of us avoid public transport altogether after dark.

Even with our own car, we are told, we cannot count on absolute security. What if it breaks down at night and we're miles from a phone? What if we have to park it several dark and dangerous yards from our destination? What if we give a lift to an innocuous-looking stranger who turns nasty? The tragic case of Marie Wilks, murdered on the M50 in June 1988, starkly underlines the helplessness of a woman who appears to have acted very sensibly.

But are things really that bad? Is there nothing for it but for us to stay at home or have a companion with us when we travel? Certainly not. For a start, as with every other type of violence against women, media coverage conveys a grossly inflated picture. Marie Wilks was a tragic case, but she was also a *one-off*. Moreover, there are many positive courses of action we can take to ensure that fear of travel doesn't impose an unjust curfew on the female half of the population.

This chapter examines the different modes of transport we use, and shows what we can do to make them more secure.

Basic precautions for public transport – trains and buses

Many women rely on public transport to get them home at night, and if you work or go out late, the journey can be scary. Most of your fellow-travellers mean you no harm, but it's foolish not to be 100 per cent alert to danger. This isn't a time for dreaming. Look out especially for the signs of drunkenness and drug abuse – perfectly innocuous people undergo dangerous personality and behavioural changes when under the influence of alcohol and drugs. Give a wide a berth to anyone you suspect of drinking and/or drug-taking.

The following precautions are your best allies on the majority of journeys. If you have teenage children who travel alone, it's imperative that they observe these rules too:

Trains (BR or underground)

- Know your local timetable so that you don't have to wait around unnecessarily.
- Wait for your train at the ticket-barrier end of the platform, and near other passengers (preferably women). Don't wander down to the far end where you may be followed by a pest.
- Never choose an empty carriage/compartment; try and sit with other women and close to a door.
- On the tube, choose the carriage nearest the guard (if there is a guard).
- If possible, choose a carriage which will draw up close to the exit at your destination.
- If a rowdy gang gets on to your part of the train, don't hang around for trouble – change carriages immediately.
- If you are bothered by someone, complain as soon as you can to the guard or driver. Alternatively, if it happens when you're in a packed compartment, complain loudly.

- If you're attacked, try to grab the emergency cord – on the tube, it's best to wait (if you can) until the train pulls into the next station.
- Try to arrange for someone to pick you up at the other end – ideally you should phone in advance so that you don't have to wait at your destination.
- If you're picking up your car, try to ensure it's as close to the station as possible – think about this when you park it in the morning.
- If you have small children with you, don't let them wander off alone.

Buses

- Know your local timetable.
- Try to avoid isolated bus stops, and stand near a street light if you can.
- If the bus stop is enclosed, it's safer to stand outside it – unless there are lots of other people around.
- Always sit downstairs, near the driver or conductor and other women.
- If a rowdy gang gets on, it may be worth considering getting off immediately – don't wait for trouble to erupt if you see it coming.
- If someone pesters you, complain to the driver or conductor.
- If you have small children with you, don't let them wander off alone.

In both buses and trains, it's advisable to keep your clothing as neutral as possible – you don't want to draw attention to yourself. If you've been out partying, wear a long coat. A friend of mine with very long, very blond hair, says she always feels much safer tucking it in under her collar.

Lobbying to improve public transport and the infrastructure

It's unjust that *we* are forced to take these precautions when the cause of the problem lies elsewhere, a twofold cause for which long-term solutions are required. The inadequacy and aggression of a minority of men is the ill for which society needs to find a cure. But society also needs to look at its infrastructure and the way in which this frequently prejudices the security of women. Nowhere is this particular evil more plain than in our public transport and affiliated systems.

Consider London Underground as an example. The mechanisation of the system has led to a reduction in staff levels. But while automatic ticket barriers may be cheaper than men in uniform, they are not as effective a deterrent to crime – in fact, they are no deterrent at all. The safety of railway travellers is being jeopardised by increased mechanisation.

Bus stops are another example. They are frequently – and unnecessarily – located in dark and isolated spots. What's to prevent them from being situated next to street lamps rather than in the dark stretches in between? Why, in many rural areas, do we still have those closed-in bus shelters which can hide the criminal from sight? And while convenience and the flow of traffic are often factors in the planning of urban bus routes, security seems to be of no account.

Another example of poor planning comes from Sevenoaks in Kent, where the street lamps go out before the arrival of the last London train. Passengers returning home by foot are obliged to negotiate the shadows. Surely if they were vocal enough, the local people could persuade their council to give them that extra hour or so of light? Similar dangerous absurdities can be found all over the country.

Acting together for change

By joining local transport users' groups, we can press for change and point out to the powers-that-be the issues that matter to us. Many of the hazards we face are quite unnecessary. It may be that the local bus company has never thought about security when siting its shelters; and councils do change their policies on all sorts of issues if they know enough people want change – it's good for votes!

One effective route of protest is via the police. If nothing else, they can furnish you with a crime profile of your area which you can use to back up your campaign. The police also have an interest in knowing where you feel at risk, and in reducing that risk. So in most communities you will find they actively support you.

In any case, you should try to bombard as many agencies as you can with your protest. The more people you pester, the more likely you are to get action. Why not involve the local newspaper and/or radio station? They're always on the lookout for strong local stories. Remember that as individuals we have limited power to force change, but banded together in groups we can achieve much to improve the conditions under which we travel.

The power of protest is illustrated by the success of London Regional Passengers Committee (a statutory body reporting to Parliament) in its campaign against staff reduction on the London Underground. The committee has argued that passenger safety is jeopardised and there are signs that LRT will change its policy.

Eight other statutory bodies have been set up by Parliament nationwide. Known as Transport Users Consultative Committees, they are there to represent and deal with the complaints of British Rail passengers, but they can also provide information about other local transport user groups. Their numbers are listed in Useful Addresses.

Taxis and minicabs

Taxis are one of the safest forms of transport around, and the security they offer can compensate for the expense. If you're working late, it's worth trying to get a cab home or to the station at company expense – responsible employers will readily agree. And in any other late-night situation, whatever your age or status, you should always consider the taxi option – after a party or an evening out, perhaps you can share the cost with friends who are going in the same direction? Ask the driver to wait until you're safely through your front door.

Mothers should impress upon older children that they must always call a *licensed* taxi or minicab if they are stuck for a lift

GETTING FROM A TO B – SAFELY

home at night – if necessary, you will pay the fare when they arrive. Mothers with small children should also consider taking a taxi if, for example, they find themselves out much later than they'd intended, laden with prams, shopping and what have you. Even if you generally travel quite happily by public transport, it can be worth it – once in a while – to incur the extra expense of a taxi to ensure your safety and that of your family.

It's always best to use black or licensed cabs, but if you have to use a mini-cab, you and your family should take some basic precautions.

- Use only firms you know and trust, or whom you've had recommended by other women.
- Never pick up a minicab on the street – the driver could be anyone.
- When you order the cab, insist you are told the driver's name, as well as the make, colour and registration of his car, and explain that you will wait indoors. All this will hinder the passing shark from posing as your driver.
- If you're phoning from a public place, it's especially important to check these details. Anyone else overhearing your call could pose as your driver and thus get you into their car.
- If the driver behaves suspiciously, don't hang around for trouble – get out of the car at the earliest opportunity.

It's worth knowing that London minicab drivers need only hold a driving licence, and that no authority checks on their background or even the safety of their car. Elsewhere, checks are at the discretion of local authorities. So, calling a minicab is really no different from hitching a lift with a stranger. Now that so many cars are fitted with central locking and childproof locks, it's often impossible to make a quick escape. The government is currently backing research into attacks on women by bogus cab drivers, the results of which may force the introduction of new legislation.

Women-only minicab firms (for women, driven by women) are still a rarity, but a London firm called Ladycabs is providing a safe service in the capital. Their number is supplied in Useful Addresses.

In your own car

If you have a car, you're lucky – from the point of view of personal security, it's your safest means of getting about. Although as drivers we may fear the recklessness of others on the road, we rarely fear attack. With the doors locked, we feel safe from harm in our private mobile fortresses.

There are, notwithstanding, a number of situations where drivers can be incredibly vulnerable, and it's therefore important to look at these.

Car parks

Basic precautions can protect us from risk in the most unpromising situations (e.g. having to return to a multi-storey car park after dark). It's imperative that we make these precautions as much a part of our driving routine as fastening our seatbelts.

Parking
• When parking, try and and imagine what the spot will be like when you return to the car. If necessary, spend time looking for a place near a light/exit etc.
• Back into your space so that you can get away swiftly.
• Lock all the doors, close all windows and remove valuables from sight.
• Memorise where you've left your car – invent a helpful rhyme if needs be.
• If you have small children with you, hold on to them tightly – you won't want to lose them here.

Leaving
• Have your keys ready in your hand or pocket, as well as a personal alarm and torch if it's dark.
• If there's an attendant, tell him you're going to fetch your car, and would he please listen out for your personal alarm.
• Walk briskly and confidently, in the middle of the traffic aisles and away from parked cars.

- Check there's no one in the back of your car before you get in.
- Again, don't let small children wander off between the aisles of cars.

Breakdowns

The Marie Wilks case chilled the hearts of all women drivers. There can be few of us who haven't asked ourselves what we would do if *we* were to break down on the motorway with two children in the car. Marie Wilks left her car and the children, walked 700 yards and phoned for help – should she have done otherwise? Here was a woman who apparently took the sensible course of action and who none the less fell victim to a brutal and fatal attack.

Before giving in to fear of driving alone, we must bear in mind that what happened to Marie Wilks is extremely rare – which is why it hit the headlines. Men like her killer are fortunately very few and very far between. We must also consider that although Marie *did* take sensible steps, there may have been other preventive measures she could have taken. For instance, had she known more about her car, she might have stopped earlier and at a service station. We will never know exactly what happened on that hard shoulder of the M50, but we must not let it 'prove' to us or anyone else that driving alone is a risky business for women.

How, then, can we improve our security when we get into our car? A few preparatory steps are essential:

- Keep all your doors locked when driving.
- *Know* and look after your car. Have it serviced regularly, and familiarise yourself with the basic tasks, such as checking tyre pressures and oil and water levels, and changing wheels.
- Always keep a jerrycan of petrol in the boot.
- Never let your fuel gauge drop below the quarter-full mark.
- Equip yourself with good maps, and plan your routes before you set off – lost drivers are vulnerable drivers.

- Keep a first-aid kit, de-icer and a personal alarm and a torch in your car.
- An aerosol of instant puncture sealant will enable you to drive on in case of puncture in an isolated spot – emergencies only!
- Keep some loose change at hand for phone calls.
- Keep a large mac, a hat and wellies in the boot at all times – if it's raining when you break down, you'll be glad of their protection. They have the additional benefit of concealing your female form from passing opportunists, and are especially comforting if you are glamorously dressed.
- Join one of the motoring organizations (details supplied in Useful Addresses).
- If your job requires a lot of solo driving, ask your employer for a car phone. Or consider buying one yourself. They can be reassuring.

Taking the above precautions will reduce the likelihood of breakdown and the attendant risks. And if your car *does* play up, you'll feel much more confident. But what do you do next? Do you stay in the car or leave it? Do you phone for help or wait? No advice will be absolutely right for every situation, and your reaction will depend as much upon who you are as upon where you are, what time of day it is and so forth.

However, the following measures seem to me the most sensible in the majority of motorway breakdowns:

- If you sense trouble, drive to an emergency phone before your car becomes undriveable.
- Keep a look-out while phoning, and tell the operator you're a woman and on your own – you'll get priority attention.
- If anyone stops to offer help (other than the police, the AA or RAC), tell them the police are on the way. If the person acts suspiciously, don't be embarrassed to recite his car details down the phone (even if you haven't yet got through to the operator!) – it should make him think twice about bothering you.

- If you have to walk to a phone, switch on the hazard lights and lock the doors. Put on a large coat (see above) to neutralise your appearance and follow the motorway markers to the nearest phone. Note the number of the marker nearest to your car for reference. Take any children with you and return to your car as quickly as possible.

- If someone pulls in as you are walking back from the phone, tell him the police are on the way. If you're *heading* for the phone and he's worrying you, let him stop his car before you start walking – even running – back to your car. By the time he gets out, you'll have a head start, and you've made things difficult for him – steal a glance at his registration, if you can.

- *Never* accept a lift to the phone.

- It's never advisable to wait in your car – 30 per cent of all motorway fatalities occur on the hard shoulder. If you can bear it, you're far safer sitting on the bank. Turn on the hazard lights and lock all doors save the front passenger door – you can jump back into the car quickly if someone draws up to 'help' you. This also applies if it's dark, and you prefer waiting to walking to a phone. Never leave children in the car.

- If a stranger does stop, speak to him through a small slit in the window and tell him the police are on their way (even if you aren't sure of this). You may consider buying a fake car phone if the real thing is beyond your means. A quick 'I'm calling the police' will rid you of most pests.

What if you break down in the middle of nowhere at night? Many of the suggestions above would still apply, and the only real difference is that a phone is less likely to be at hand. But it's still your best bet – you could wait in your car for hours without any real help passing by.

Again, you should know your car, and stop at a garage or phone as soon as there are signs of trouble –

Never take the risk of pushing on to your destination.

Try to take note of phones as you drive along, so that if you *do* break down, you have an idea of how far back you'll have to walk. It's better to walk back to a pub or village you've passed and where you know there's a phone, than forward where there may not be one for several miles.

More than ever, you'll be glad of your torch and a big, warm and form-disguising coat. Always have them in your car. If someone suspicious does stop as you are walking along the road, tell him the police are on their way and that your husband is just behind/ahead of you. You have to believe you can lie convincingly so think *now* of what you would say – and practise it.

Pest drivers

These are the bullies who drive up beside you, try to nudge you off the road, race you and sometimes follow you. I know that they can be terrifying: four youths came up beside me once on the M1, and tried to get me to race them. When I refused to play ball, they overtook me, crossed my bows, moved into the inside lane and jeered me from the other side. I was very alarmed and grimly drove on, refusing to look at them or respond. Unwittingly, I had adopted the best tactic, for they soon grew bored with me and drove off.

But what else can we do to avoid these people and the threat they represent? Again, there is much we can do to help ourselves:

- If your route is a regular one, *learn it*. Where could you get help if you needed it? Should you vary it from time to time?
- Don't draw attention to your vehicle – avoid silly stickers, furry animals and anything else that tells strangers you're cute or game for a laugh.
- Ignore any driver who acts aggressively – any form of acknowledgement will be read as encouragement.
- If ignoring the man doesn't work, try heading for a busy place where you can get help. The local police station's the best option.
- On a motorway, you may have to resort to flashing your lights and sounding your horn, thereby alerting other drivers to your problem.

- If he manages to overtake you and block your route forward, stay in the car. Once he gets out of his car and starts walking towards you, you can reverse, turn and drive away.

On any longish journey it's always wise to tell someone at your destination what time you plan to arrive. Tell them your route, too. Knowing someone's expecting you and ready to raise the alarm is a great source of comfort if things do go wrong en route.

And three final points for women drivers:

- *Never* give lifts to strangers.
- If you're flagged down (even by those who appear to be the law), stay in your car and speak through a slit in the window.
- *Most important* – if you can give a lift to girlfriends or female colleagues, do so. We can be quite selfish about our cars, and often it only requires us to go five minutes out of our way to save another woman the anxiety of a bus or train ride home.

Security courses for women drivers

Many firms now seek expert advice for employees who spend much of their time on the road. One of the most popular and useful courses available is the Women's Mobile Security Course run by Mike Reed of Driving Management Ltd – it is also the only course designed specifically for women concerned about their security when on the road. Details are supplied in Useful Addresses.

A note on car security

Your car is a valuable possession, and one that you should protect. Nearly 400,000 cars go missing in Britain each year, and a quarter of those are never recovered. Here's how you can look after yours:

- Don't leave anything of value on display (e.g. briefcases, shopping, photographic equipment) – lock it all in the boot and discourage opportunists.
- If you're driving in hot weather with your windows open, tuck your handbag and other valuables away from view.
- Lock your car whenever you leave it – even if it's only for a few minutes.
- Etch your windows, hi-fi system and lights with a code of your own. Either do the job yourself, or ask for help from your garage or local police station. Display a sticker informing potential thieves of this precaution.
- Ensure your fuel cap is lockable.
- Fit lockable wheel nuts.
- Buy a toughened steel steering wheel hook – this is a better deterrent than the built-in steering locks.
- Have your car code-marked. Even after a respray it will be traceable. Display a sticker informing thieves of this precaution.
- Consider having an alarm fitted.

Summary

Travelling can expose us to threat – if no precautions are taken. This chapter has examined the ways in which we can reduce that threat, and thereby maintain our freedom to go where we please, and when. The key points are summarised in the checklist below.

Trains and buses

- Know your timetables.
- Try to avoid waiting on deserted platforms or at isolated stops.
- Take basic precautions such as sitting with other women and/or near the driver/guard.
- Move away from potential troublemakers.

- Give a wide berth to drunks or drug abusers.

- Complain loudly if you're molested.

- If there's an emergency cord, don't be afraid to use it.

- Think about your destination – can you arrange to be met? Is your car parked close by? Try to think in advance about these things – especially if you're travelling at night.

- Keep your appearance as neutral as possible.

- Keep small children close to you.

- Impress all these points on children who travel alone.

- Lobby to improve public transport – joint a local transport users' group, elicit the support of police and media, bully your local authority and transport bodies.

Taxis

- Choose a black cab over a minicab.

- Use only minicab firms you know – at least by repute.

- Never pick up a minicab in the street.

- Insist on driver and cab details when you order a minicab.

- Wait for the cab indoors.

- If the driver behaves suspiciously, get out at the first opportunity – don't worry about appearing rude.

- Tell your children they can always get a licensed taxi if they're stuck somewhere – you'll pay. Impress all the other points on them.

Your own car

- Avoid breakdowns by knowing and looking after your car.

- Take security measures to protect your car from theft.

- Take basic precautions such as keeping a can of petrol in your car.

- Take special precautions in large multi-storey car parks – such as parking near an exit, memorising exactly where you left your car and keeping an alert eye open for suspicious characters.

- Have good maps and plan your routes – in advance.

- Keep a large mac, hat and wellies in the boot.

- Join a motoring organisation.

- On the motorway, stop at the first phone if you sense trouble.

- Tell the operator you are a woman alone/with children.

- Don't accept help or lifts from strangers.

- Don't wait inside the car – a third of all motorway fatalities occur on the hard shoulder.

- If you break down on a country road, walk *back* to the nearest phone you remember – only walk forward if you know that there's a closer phone ahead of you.

- Ignore pest drivers – if that doesn't work, head for the nearest busy place and get help.

- On all long journeys tell someone your estimated time of arrival and your route.

- If you're flagged down, stay in the car and speak only through a slit in the window – until you're sure this really is the police.

- Be generous in giving lifts to other women.

CHAPTER 6

Resisting Attack

Preparing for attack

So far this book has been about preventing attack. It has looked at the importance of awareness and assertiveness, and it has shown that we all have the power to protect ourselves from threat both to our person and our property. We do not have to live in fear, we do not in fact have to stop *living* in any sense of the word.

This does not mean, however, that we can make ourselves one hundred per cent invulnerable to attack – the best security money could buy didn't prevent the near-successful attempts on the lives of Pope John Paul and Ronald Reagan, or the assassination of President Kennedy. We all have to be prepared for the worst. Each one of us has to address the question of how we could cope under attack. Part of our new strength must be drawn from the knowledge that were we to be attacked we would be resourceful, we would defend ourselves, we would get away. We would not – above all else – submit ourselves to 'fate'.

Revising old attitudes

Before discussing the strategies to adopt under attack, we need to look hard at our attitudes. As discussed in Chapter 1, we've long been fed the images of the woman who freezes, who acquiesces or who, at best, screams when threatened. All that must go – re-read the chapter, if necessary, to remind yourself of the ways in which you can learn that assertiveness essential to any programme for self-protection.

We will only succeed in defending ourselves if we absolutely believe that we have every chance of getting away. We are neither feeble nor helpless. As David and Goliath so usefully proved, brawn isn't everything.

Resisting the 'freeze'

Attackers want and expect their attack to be quick and without complication. The element of surprise is on their side, and they assume a stunned lack of resistance from their target. This rule is as applicable to flashers as it is to muggers, men who follow you in the street, intruders in the night and any other pest or violent attacker. Remember it.

Anything the target – i.e. *you* – can do to shake this set of assumptions will instantly weaken the attacker's advantage.

You must surprise him. Pre-empting and avoiding the attack, yelling in anger, shouting 'No!', struggling, fleeing, kicking, even biting – these are all positive reactions which will surprise and wrong-foot the criminal. They are the positive and achievable alternative to the freeze.

Unfortunately, freezing is the classic and shocked response of most people when attacked (men and women alike), and many victims who have tried to scream or react in any other way have reported that they simply couldn't. As the victim, you are taken completely by surprise by this unknown and unexpected aggressor. At first you simply cannot register that the attack is happening to you – these things only happen to other people. By the time you have taken stock of the situation, it's too late – by freezing you've lost the chance of gaining any sort of advantage over your attacker.

Given how rarely we are called upon to deal with this sort of situation, it's not surprising our responses are slow. But by preparing ourselves ahead of time, thinking through in advance how we would respond positively to danger, we can sharpen our responses and reduce the likelihood of the 'freeze'.

A passive response to danger is *not* safer

Women are frequently advised that a passive response is safer, that they should 'go' with the attack in the hopes that nothing worse will happen. This maddens me, for it rather presumes that a 'successful' mugging or rape doesn't in itself result in physical and mental injury. It also implies some sort of bizarre bargain with the criminal: you let him have his way, he promises not to hurt you more than he 'has to'. Yet what basis do you have to trust this man to honour the bargain?

In any attack you have only yourself to trust. You have to decide now that any attack – however minor – is an outrage you will not tolerate and that it could result in severe injury if you do not act to defend yourself. The following measures will help you react *actively* in the moment of stress:

- Be angry and show it – this man has *no right* to intrude on your person.
- Believe that you *can* defend yourself.
- Arm yourself with self-protection strategies so that your belief is well-founded.
- Be committed to any self-defence measures you take.
- Think about and practise these strategies *now*, so that you are well-prepared for the moment of stress.

Strategies for self-defence

Research carried out very recently in the United States has proved that the women who actively resist rape are the ones who also avoid it – there was no proof that the passive response was effective. In their book *Stopping Rape* (Pergamon) Pauline Bart and Patricia O'Brien conclude that **'the best overall advice we could offer women to increase the probability of avoiding rape is "Don't be a nice girl".'** It seems logical to suggest that the same might also apply to other types of attack.

Research has also proved beyond all reasonable doubt that those who actively resist their aggressor survive their ordeal with fewer psychological scars. Guilt can be one of the heaviest burdens a victim bears after an attack, and you are likely to suffer more acutely if you know you did not fight back. Active resistance is a means of maintaining your self-esteem.

Fighting back does not necessarily involve actual physical violence, although you may have to resort to this (the most effective moves are described in the Appendix). There are several other ways in which we can defend ourselves – and we can apply the following basic principles to most situations:

- Fleeing/walking away from danger.
- Keeping a diary and gathering as much evidence as you can, before taking the matter to the police or perhaps (if at work) your superiors.
- Making a lot of noise (either with your lungs or a screech alarm) so as to attract attention to your plight and alarm the attacker.
- Talking to him – reasoning with him, stalling him, conning him.
- Pretending to play along while you wait for him to drop his guard (particularly relevant when he is armed).
- Physical force.

The course of action you take will depend upon the attack, the attacker and upon you – it will be up to you to make the decision about how you defend yourself at the moment of attack. It's likely that you'll have to use more than one of the above strategies.

Examples of positive resistance to aggression

At the risk of being repetitive, I must reassert that there is no blueprint for resisting an attack, no 'model' procedure. Every attacker, every target of an attack, is going to be different. And in the final count every individual must make her own decision about how best to defend herself.

The following examples do, however, demonstrate the active ways in which women can and do protect themselves. A positive pattern of behaviour emerges and the best anyone can do is adapt that pattern to her needs.

1. Rachel (Avoidance)

Rachel is walking home late at night, and hears male footsteps behind her. She feels uncomfortable, even afraid. Her instincts scream at her that this man spells trouble, but because she has been trained to *inaction*, she keeps on walking and does not take immediate and decisive steps to avert danger.

What positive steps might she take?

- Rachel could cross the road, to begin with. By doing so, she immediately puts a more comfortable distance between herself and the stranger.
- If he follows her across, and there is no apparent reason why he should do so other than that he's a pest, she should cross again – decisively and without breaking into a panicky run. No? Why not? It certainly grates against our in-bred manners, but good manners aren't relevant where survival's concerned.
- By crossing for a second, third, even fourth time, she is stating that she knows he's there and that she does not want trouble. *She is removing from him the element of surprise – his most deadly weapon.* Opportunists will certainly be deterred, and those actively seeking a 'victim' will have a clear message that Rachel is not 'victim' material. The strategy she has employed is avoidance of danger.

Many women may think that crossing the street to avoid a man or group of men indicates neurosis and fear. To you it may well feel that way, but so long as you walk with a firm step, moving always with purpose, you will be giving off very strong 'don't mess with me' signals. The majority of attackers avoid people like you.

In a situation like Rachel's, where you are being followed, there may be other strategies of avoidance/flight:

- Do you know anyone living in the street whose doorbell you could ring?
- Are there any shops, pubs or other public places nearby?
- Is there a better-lit street you can turn into?

Whatever course of action she takes, Rachel should turn at least once and get a good, long look at the man. Even if she's not 100 per cent sure that he was following her, she should report him to the police – it may prevent him from harming or frightening another woman or child. A detailed description is therefore imperative. If he's following her in a car, she should take mental note of the registration – the police can run immediate checks on their computer.

2. Liz (Avoidance)

In another, quite different situation, the same tactics of avoidance apply.

> Liz is in a multi-storey car park, heading up the stairs to where her car is parked. Her daughter, aged five, is hanging on to her hand. Liz sees a group of youths loitering ahead of her, they're making a lot of noise, and she simply *knows* she does not want to walk past them.

She should:

- Turn round and walk briskly but calmly back.
- If she really feels this is so 'obvious', she should pretend she's forgotten something – she could say something like, 'Oh dear, mummy's forgotten to buy her magazine. We'll have to go back for it.'

Whatever she does, Liz shouldn't walk into danger if she senses it's there. She should learn to trust her instincts and get away while it's easy to do so – an early reaction is all the more vital when she's with a child. She should never simply walk on into potential trouble against her better judgement. By being imaginative and alert, she is turning her fear into positive action.

This strategy of avoidance can be applied to any potentially dangerous situation. It is the most useful strategy we can employ and will usually deflect the need for any further action. It relies on believing in our gut reactions – something we are rather bad at doing. At times it may mean that we assign vile motives to the innocent, and we may even make fools of ourselves. But isn't that better than the alternative?

3. Becky (Flight/avoidance followed by yelling)

Like Rachel, Becky is being followed in the street. She has crossed the road several times and failed to shake off the pest. She realizes he means business. There's nowhere for her to get help, and she now has to act. Her best option is to yell aggressively at the man, telling him to get lost. She should be uncomprising, showing him her outrage, and demonstrating that she will not stand for his behaviour. Facing him will also give her the chance of a good long look at the pest – which will be invaluable when she goes to the police.

Yelling at strangers in the street goes against the grain of what's deemed acceptable female behaviour, but frankly such niceties are utterly irrelevant. The important thing now is to shake off this nuisance before he becomes a real danger.

Everything we know about men who attack women they have never met before shows they *are* deterred when their intended victim yells.

In three separate incidents, girlfriends of mine swung round on the man they were being followed by, and shouted at him to go away. Two of the three pests swore back and one aggressively denied any intent . . . but in each case, they disappeared from the scene quite swiftly.

Yelling is a tactic which can prove surprisingly difficult to master. It is a truism to say that we freeze under attack, and that includes a freezing of the vocal chords. One way of loosening them is by *practising* shouting, yelling, etc. – as suggested in Chapter 1. Screaming tends to be a defensive and rather female noise, so try to develop a really aggressive yell instead.

As with every other strategy for self-protection, however, the best cure for the freeze is a new and positive attitude – a belief that bellowing at an attacker is neither an embarrassing nor a stupid thing to do – and it may draw the attention of passers-by to your plight.

4. Anna (Yelling)

Anna is at a cashpoint machine. She is alone, it is dark and the street is ill-lit. A block away she sees the comforting lights of a pub with people standing outside. She takes the precaution of keeping her bag held tight against her body, and she keeps a vigilant eye on the street behind her as she carries out her transaction. A man suddenly appears from the shadows and grabs hold of her. What should she do?

- Anna's best bet is to yell as loud as she can. She must scare the aggressor and tell anybody about that she needs their help – and fast.

The trouble is, people are generally loathe to become involved when they hear the noise of a male-female struggle, and one of the most disturbing aspects of violent attack is that it's frequently carried out under the incurious noses of our fellow-citizens. It's easy to assume you're friends or lovers just having a friendly tussle, or, that you're involved in a domestic dispute. People don't automatically assume that there's a rape or mugging going on right before their eyes. And even if they do, they are often unsure about what best they can do. Horrible though it may sound, it's easier to walk on by.

- In Anna's situation, where there are people within hearing distance, she should overcome their natural resistance to involvement by shouting 'Fire!' or giving simple and specific instructions – 'Call the police!', for example.
- She should keep repeating this over and over (if she can), and not be worn down by a lack of reaction. The chances are that even if help fails to materialise, the racket she's making will frighten the attacker, and at any moment he may decide he should split. His ultimate goal, after all, is *not* to get caught.

- If he is determined to have her bag, she should let it go. It is never worth getting hurt for the sake of a few possessions.

5. Ruth (Talking, pretending to play along with the attacker, physical force, flight)

Ruth, who is 72, woke up to find a man standing by her bed, a knife in his hand. She doesn't know where she found the presence of mind, but her first action was to offer him a cup of tea. She realised he intended to rape and perhaps kill her, and that her only means of self-protection was to keep the man talking until his guard dropped.

She was terrified, but managed to persuade him to come into the kitchen. 'We'll have a cup of tea first, she kept saying, 'and then we can go to bed.' She flattered the man, and told him she wanted to go to bed with him, but that she would like to have a cup of tea first. The man sat down in the kitchen, visibly relaxing. Ruth filled the teapot with boiling water, brought it over to the man and, to his astonishment, smashed it over his head. Without stopping to see the results of her action, she hurried out of her flat and banged on her neighbour's door. Her neighbour telephoned the police.

The strategy of talking to an assailant or potential assailant is not appropriate in most situations. If, for example, a car draws up next to yours and the driver shouts an obscenity through the window, it's best to remain silent and ignore him. Any smart reply may be read as encouragement, absurd though that may seem, and lead to further trouble. Likewise, in a situation like Rachel's, you clearly do not want to engage the man in any sort of conversation – even if it is tempting to tell him what you think of him.

If, however, he has you pinned to the ground, with a knife at your throat, the situation is dramatically different. Talking may be your only route to survival. Plead, cajole, reason – but whatever you do, keep him talking and play for time. The object here is not so much to make him change his mind (clearly this is desirable, but not a realistic hope). What you're doing is waiting for that split second when he may relax his hold on you or drop his guard, and that's when you make your bid to escape (usually using one or more of the self-defence moves described in the Appendix).

6. Tilly (Keeping a diary)

Tilly is a widow in her sixties. For years she cleaned for the elderly woman who lived next door with her middle-aged son. When the woman died, Tilly continued to clean the house for the son. One day he exposed himself to her in the bathroom. Tilly, appalled, hit him with a towel and refused to enter his house again.

There followed a campaign of sexual harassment which increased in severity with every week that passed. First the man would flash at Tilly over the garden fence, then he began entering her garden at night, rustling the bushes to terrify her. She became really frightened when he took to flashing at her through the window at night and making obscene phone calls.

Tilly was sceptical about the police and she therefore noted in a diary every incident. She kept the diary for nearly three months. She then showed it to the police who took action to protect her from further harassment. At the time, the police admitted there was little they could have done in the early stages and that by biding her time and keeping the diary, Tilly had presented them with the strongest possible case against the man.

A note on using physical force

You do not have to be stronger than your assailant in order to get the better of him in a fight (as Ruth's story should demonstrate), but you must be prepared to fight dirty and then to get out quick. The aim is to inflict as much pain as you can so that your attacker releases you. The techniques (illustrated in the Appendix) are basic: biting, kicking, bending back fingers and so forth.

Physical force is often recommended only as a last resort, and by and large I would go with this – shout and run first, and don't get involved in a fight unless you absolutely have to.

A case where force is really your only option might be where a man grabs you from behind. If you keep your wits about you, and if you've thought in advance about all the natural weapons at your disposal, you can hurt him in a number of ways: you can throw your head back, bashing the hard mound of your skull against his very vulnerable nose; you can bite hard into his hand; stamp your stiletto or heel hard on to the bridge of his foot; kick his shins; swing your elbow back into his solar plexus; grab hold of his little fingers and pull them back until they snap.

You must go for the vulnerable spots, and you must go for them *hard* first time round. You have to hurt him badly enough for him to release you, if only momentarily. That's when you run, yelling your head off as you go.

As I have said, the most effective techniques are also the most basic. Many women choose to join a local self-defence class in order to learn more sophisticated moves. This is certainly no bad thing, as it raises their awareness, self-confidence and general level of fitness. My only reservation about the self-defence industry (and it comes in a host of different guises) is that women can come away from their classes with an inflated idea of their own fighting abilities. Being able to throw a female partner in class is quite different from being able to throw an aggressive and unco-operative male assailant. However prepared you are, you are unlikely to be prepared enough. There's another danger too: women who have been training may become more involved in a dangerous fight than necessary. It's often the swift, basic, unsophisticated knee in the groin (which requires no formal training) that does the trick best.

Perhaps more than any other aspect of self-protection, the use of physical force requires forethought and practice. As women we are squeamish about violence, and loathe to inflict pain even on those who mean us harm. We need to overcome our instinctive pacifism, by learning to respond with anger to aggression. Once that anger is released, we are as capable as anyone of hurting someone else when we have to.

Summary

The purpose of this chapter has been to show the many ways in which women can and do defend themselves when attacked. The traditional passive response is inappropriate and dangerous. We need to replace it with action. The principal points are listed below:

- Be prepared for attack – no one is invulnerable.

- Believe that however bad your situation may seem, there are always ways in which you can get the better of the aggressor.

- Justify that belief by arming yourself with strategies, and thinking in advance how you would use them under stress.

- Remember that a passive 'freeze' is rarely safer – research shows that women who resist rape (for example) also avoid it.

- You will suffer less from post-attack guilt and loss of self-esteem if you know you actively resisted your attacker.

- Any positive response from you (yelling, kicking, fleeing, etc.) will surprise the attacker, and so give you an advantage.

- Be angry – **no one has the right to hurt you**.

- Be prepared to give up property (e.g. a handbag) rather than get hurt.

- Be committed to any self-defensive action you take – this applies especially to physical force, where you cannot afford to be half-hearted in your efforts. You must be prepared to inflict maximum pain so as to give yourself the best chance of escaping.

CHAPTER 7

Coping with the Aftermath of an Attack

Originally, this chapter was not going to be included. This book is about prevention, and in my early plans I saw no place for post-attack considerations: they wouldn't be necessary. I was being naïve, of course. Whatever our precautions, we *may* still suffer an attack – just as tomorrow we may be struck down by disease or a drunken driver. The measures described in the previous chapters massively reduce the likelihood of attack, but nothing can eliminate it. Any book setting out to advise women on self-protection is therefore incomplete (and even irresponsible) without a section on what reactions to expect in the days, weeks and months following a violent assault, and what avenues of redress are open to you.

The chapter pays special attention to the crimes of rape and sexual assault. These hideous crimes result in the deepest level of post-attack shock, and are dealt with by a legal system which has little sympathy for women.

Shock

Many victims of attack are surprised at the intensity of the shock that follows their ordeal, and the way in which it undermines their confidence and quality of life for maybe years after the event. Even relatively minor incidents can cast a long, dark shadow over your daily existence.

It took Penny an unbelievably long time fully to recover from merely *witnessing* a violent mugging on her street: for the first month she feared walking out of the house alone – in daylight; she changed all her routes; she suffered panic attacks and palpitations whenever she passed the spot of the incident; never again did she return home late by public transport.

How much more must the victim have felt?

Amanda simply couldn't believe the degree of shock she suffered after losing her handbag to a couple of 12-year-olds. Her confidence disintegrated, and she became paranoid about leaving her flat on her own. She felt angry with herself for 'allowing' the incident to occur, and continues to blame herself (quite unjustly) for not preventing the theft.

Expecting and accepting these perfectly normal reactions is all part of the healing process. We shouldn't be astonished at the intensity of our emotions: in the worst attacks we may well have stared death in the face; and in those less serious we will still have to come to terms with having happen to us what 'only happens to other people'. In rape cases the post-attack reaction suffered by victims is now so commonly recognised that it bears the name of Rape Trauma Syndrome.

Depending on the nature of the assault, we can expect to suffer a number of different and disturbing reactions – *all of which are absolutely normal*:

- Sleeplessness and nightmares.
- A loss of interest in sex (especially in rape cases).
- Fear and panic attacks, especially when you go out alone.
- Obsessive flashbacks to the attack.
- A compulsion to talk about it or, conversely, a reluctance to talk about the attack at all.
- Tearfulness.
- In cases of rape and sexual assault, shame and hatred of your own body, which may result in obsessive washing.
- Anger, which you may take out on your loved ones.
- Loneliness and isolation.

- Feelings of futility and dull depression.
- Guilt – if only you had done this, that or the other, you might have prevented the attack.

All this, on top of the painful physical scars your ordeal may have left you with – bruising, cuts and other injuries – as well as anxiety about the possibility of pregnancy or sexually trans-mitted infections in cases of rape and sexual assault. Is it really so surprising that it takes time to make a complete recovery from the shock? Even Penny said it took about three months for her to recover from witnessing an assault. Ride the shock and let it take its course. Do not believe for a minute that it is weak, wrong or abnormal for you to experience any or all of these reactions.

Guilt

Guilt is possibly the most damaging of all the after-effects from which a victim of attack suffers, and one of the most common. Women who 'freeze' and find themselves unable to fight back are likely to suffer most from the feeling that somehow they were to blame. And even those who actively resist their attacker are by no means immune to feelings of guilt. *Why did I take that route home? Why didn't I listen to my instinctive warning signals?* You blame yourself unfairly, but you blame yourself none the less.

Unfortunately, the sense of guilt can be reinforced by friends, doctors, police, lawyers, judges who will ask you, typically:

- Why didn't you take a taxi?
- Why did you let him into your flat?
- Why didn't you say 'no'?
- Why did you wear such a short skirt?

Even those whom we love and trust can be prone to asking such questions, unaware that they can be deeply damaging and actually prolong the process of healing.

You are not to blame for your attack

All of these questions miss the point. *You are not responsible for the behaviour of your attacker.* He alone is the guilty party. Whatever actions you may or may not have taken, you did not ask for the assault. To suggest otherwise is absurd. Once we start blaming victims, we remove responsibility from the aggressor and, effectively, give him *carte blanche* to continue in his violent ways. It's important to hold on to this thought, as it will help you come to terms with your natural (but unjust) tendency to blame yourself. It will also give the sensitivity you will need if a friend or relative of yours is ever attacked.

How to help yourself recover

Talking to a friend

It's often helpful to talk through your ordeal and your reactions with a close friend, someone whom you can trust. Accept that you have good reason to feel this way, and share the burden with someone else – don't trivialise your trauma by saying to yourself, 'It was only a minor incident, I don't want to bore people with it.' Even 'minor' attacks can be extremely disturbing – bringing your emotions into the open helps normalise them and assists the healing process.

You may find it easier to talk to a female friend, if your attack was sexual. Not surprisingly, your feelings towards the opposite sex (even towards those men whom you love and trust) may well be ambiguous. Again, this is perfectly normal. Give yourself time, and don't feel you have to talk to your partner if you aren't ready to do so. Try not to burden yourself with anxiety about your relationship and your partner's feelings – you have been put through a violent and distressing experience and you need to heal. If your partner is understanding, he will be gentle and patient and eventually you will return to a normal sex life.

Help from the experts

Sometimes you may need expert help. There are a number of agencies – Victim Support Schemes, Rape Crisis Centres –

which provide confidential support and counselling services both for you and your loved ones who may have become secondary victims. It can be much easier to talk to a trained stranger then to a well-meaning friend or family member, and such agencies can put you in touch with people who have been through and come out the other end of bad experiences like yours. Contact numbers and addresses are supplied on pages 137–8.

Other practical measures

There are many other positive steps to be taken, which will combine to ease the pain. Each person and each attack is different, but here are some of the practical measures that might help you recover from a violent attack:

- Move house or change your phone number, if the attack was home-related.
- Change departments at work, or even your job, if the attack was related to your work.
- Become involved in local groups campaigning to improve streetlighting etc., or join a Neighbourhood Watch scheme.
- Take a holiday.
- Try to resume a normal life, and do not let your fear control you and confine you to your home.

Reporting the assault

It is a matter of deep concern that thousands of women never report crimes committed against them to the police. If the police never learn of the attack, the attacker will go free – and attack again. Burglary and theft of property are less of a problem – if nothing else, they are reported for insurance purposes. But sexual assaults and rape are another matter altogether. The figures vary, but a study for the Women's National Commission suggests that up to 75 per cent of rapes are officially unrecorded, and 75 per cent of the women who reported sexual assaults to the London Rape Crisis Centre between 1976 and 1980 did not go to the police.

There are a number of reasons why: the woman may fear that she'll be accused of consent or provocation; she may fear that she'll be told she was 'asking for it' (e.g. by accepting a lift, wearing revealing clothing or inviting a man home); she may feel ashamed; she may have been threatened with retaliation by her attacker; she may be frightened of her family's reaction (especially if she comes from a religious community); or she may have no faith in the processes of justice – by telling the police she'll prolong her ordeal for nothing.

All of these reasons are valid. Nobody should ever force a victim to report her attack if she has powerful motives for not doing so. The decision must be hers, and hers alone.

However, it's worth each of us giving some thought now to what we really believe is right. How would we act after an attack? Would we remain silent or not? From the comfort of our armchairs, it's easy for most of us to agree that reporting the crime must be right. My belief is that it's also our duty to other women, and for two reasons. The first is obvious: by not reporting the crime (and immediately), the criminal gets away with his act of violence. As one journalist recently commented in an article on the subject, '[reporting is so low that] if you are a flasher, groper or rapist, it seems it would be very bad luck indeed if you were actually caught, tried and punished.' Do we really want to encourage this attitude?

Secondly, and perhaps more importantly, by not reporting an attack we are actually trivialising the offence. We're saying that it doesn't matter that someone assaulted us. Let's pretend the assault never happened.

But how can we expect to correct the gross shortcomings of the law and its disrespect for women if we do not demonstrate that *we* – as women and potential targets – take these crimes seriously? How can we persuade the male establishment that these crimes deserve real punishment if we don't even report them?

We must not devalue the crimes or ourselves, and we must be committed to reporting them – however 'trivial' they might seem; however embarrassing or painful the follow-up might be; however slim the chances seem of redress through law.

What to expect from the police

Fear and mistrust of the police have stopped many victims of attack from going to the law, and there are countless stories of police incompetence and insensitivity which give credence to these women's misgivings. There is real evidence, however, that in the last two or three years the police have made huge efforts to change their methods and earn the public's confidence. There has been much soul-searching, a result of which was the publication in 1985 of the book *Investigating Rape – A New Approach for Police* by Ian Blair (now Deputy Chair of the Metropolitan Standing Committee on Serious Sexual Assault Against Adults). In his concluding chapter he writes: 'Urgent reform must be carried through as soon as possible, and much of the responsibility for that reform must fall on the police service.'

Although the subsequent commitment to reform has been patchy – Britain's 52 regional forces are largely autonomous – the climb in reporting figures does back up the view that police attitudes and methods are changing. In 1987, for instance, 2500 rapes were reported to the police, a figure 8 per cent higher than that of 1986, one third higher than that of 1985 and more than double the annual figure recorded between 1977 and 1981. The greater part of these rises in numbers is attributable not to a growth in crime, but to the willingness of victims to come forward.

While reporting a violent attack – and especially a sexual one – is never going to be easy, the police do seem to have taken practical steps towards making the process more bearable. In 1985, for instance, they set up the first of a series of special victim examination suites, designed to appear 'unofficial' and therefore less intimidating. The horror of the identity parade is also being phased out – albeit slowly. The gradual introduction of two-way glass means that victims can walk down the line of faces, seeing but unseen.

This new and long-overdue sensitivity to the victim's needs means that in many forces she will now be chaperoned throughout her investigation by a woman police officer, and stringent efforts will be made to locate a female doctor where a medical examination is necessary (although this last is never guaranteed). A further change is that where once she was required to make her full statement immediately (thereby spending perhaps 16–17 hours at the police station unwashed and unrested), the victim can now go home and return to complete the procedure the following day. It is now agreed that victims of violent crimes in fact give more accurate and detailed statements when they've had a chance to recover from their ordeal, so this more humane approach is beneficial all round.

The police will want to know as much as you can remember about your assailant, so get a good look at him if you can. It sounds a ridiculously tall order, but if you plan NOW the sort of details you would look for, you have a far better chance of noting them in a moment of stress.

- How tall is he?
- What colour?
- What about his voice?
- His age?
- Did he have a car? If so, what type? What registration?
- Had you ever seen him before?

If you have been raped or sexually assaulted, a medical examination may also have to be carried out immediately. It's unpleasant, but essential, that you do not wash or change your clothes beforehand, as you could remove vital clues. You will also receive advice and counselling on pregnancy and sexually transmitted diseases, and you will be booked into a VD clinic – out of hours, so as to ensure confidentiality.

As I mentioned earlier, the response of different police forces to these changes has been mixed. While everyone will have looked at the question in improving their interviewing techniques, actual improvements are not consistent. Women should, however, be encouraged by what is happening in the police force. It is only by using the system that we can expect to improve it, and going to the police remains the only route via which we can hope to stop the attacker from repeating his crime.

By remaining silent, we set him free.

The legal process in sexual attacks

You have no recourse to the law unless you report your attack to the police. If your case does go to court, your status is that of a witness and no more. It is the police who bring the case on your behalf, who appoint solicitors and barristers, and you really have very little control over what happens thereafter.

All this is another reason why so many women back away from reporting their ordeal. This, and the disheartening fact that once rapists actually get to court, one-third of them are acquitted. On average, those who are convicted spend just 20 months in prison before being released into society once more.

Many of the system's shortcomings are rooted in history and male prejudice, but there are other very complex issues at stake. In rape trials, for instance, the advent of DNA testing has proved a mixed blessing. Because the test can show beyond doubt that a sexual act has or hasn't taken place between chief witness (i.e. you) and defendant (i.e. the attacker), those accused are turning increasingly to 'consent' for defence – in other words, they will claim that you willingly took part in the sexual act, a notoriously difficult claim to disprove and especially in so-called 'date' rapes. You are talking about one person's word against another, with a jury being asked to believe a rape was committed 'beyond reasonable doubt'. Without corroborative evidence it can be difficult for a jury to reach a decision.

This places a heavy burden on the police officer in charge of your case, who must decide whether or not there is enough corroborative evidence to give a reasonable prospect of conviction. Even if the police are utterly convinced by your account of the attack, they are also well aware of the high acquittal rate and of the distress a trial will cause you, particularly one which results in the release of your assailant.

Is it worth putting you through the trauma of a court appearance – maybe several – if you stand no chance of seeing justice done? Ian Blair, in his book *Investigating Rape*, describes this Hobson's choice: 'Sooner or later you have to decide whether to proceed or not. You have to include the victim's welfare in that decision. It's probably the most difficult professional decision a policeman has to face.'

These are the depressing facts, but they should not stop us from using the law to seek redress. It may be inadequate, but it is the only alternative we have to allowing the criminal uncontested freedom. If we are determined to take our case to court, and the police are not prepared to support us (perhaps for the reasons described above), we can take private action through the civil courts. The two immediate shortcomings here are the cost and loss of the anonymity guaranteed by law in police prosecutions for sexual offences – your name and face could be splashed across the papers. Consequently private action remains relatively rare. If your attack was suffered at work, your employer may provide you with the necessary financial and legal support for private action.

There is much we can do as individuals to improve the system for the future. Rather than shunning the law because of its inadequacies, we should be angered into action. Lobby your MP on specifics: the appointment of more women judges; the stiffening of sentences for sexual offenders; changes in the law, such as the right of the victim to appeal against an inadequate sentence; the allocation and earmarking of more money for police training, victim examination suites and so forth. These are all issues that matter, and they're worth fighting for. Sitting back and complaining that the system is unjust will never bring about the changes we need.

A note on compensation

Compensation for injury from assault is available from magistrates courts and from the Criminal Injuries Compensation scheme. Although failure to report your assault does not debar you from compensation, you're more likely to be considered favourably if you have been to the police (a conviction is not necessary). You have to make your claim within three years of the attack. Currently, the minimum award stands at £400, and awards are reduced to take account of social security payments, employer's pension and certain types of insurance. At the time

COPING WITH THE AFTERMATH OF AN ATTACK

of going to press, substantial awards may result in withdrawal of all social security benefits. This last is another issue over which many people feel strongly, and is a further area for campaigning: reinstatement of benefits would vastly improve the lot of victims.

Further information about compensation and the necessary application forms are available from the Criminal Injuries Compensation Board, the address of which is supplied on page 137.

Support agencies

The National Association of Victim Support Schemes is an expanding voluntary service with trained counsellors in most areas. They are there to befriend you and help you recover. Your local police station will put you in touch with your nearest branch. Alternatively, you can contact head office. Their address is on page 138.

Rape Crisis Centres are autonomous groups set up across the country, which offer a varied service. Many provide a 24-hour phone line, and all share a commitment to helping and supporting women through the trauma of sexual assault. Your local number should be obtainable through Directory Enquiries. The principal centres are listed on pages 138.

Summary

Victims of attack suffer from shock that may last for many months. This chapter has tried to outline the reactions you can expect after a violent assault, and has described ways in which you can overcome the trauma. It also looks at how police deal with sexual attacks on women, and the legal process which remains our only vehicle of redress.

The following points summarise the chapter:

- Don't be surprised by the intensity of your post-attack shock – even relatively minor incidents can take months to recover from.

- Try not to blame yourself. However careless you may have been. you did not ask to be attacked. **Victims are never guilty.**

- Talk through the ordeal with a friend or with experts.

- After a sexual attack, do not be surprised if you feel ambivalent about your partner. Give yourself time to heal, and seek help from experts if necessary.

- You may need to take drastic practical steps in order to restore normality to your life – e.g. by moving house. Be prepared to take them.

- Report your assault to the police. Without them, you have no recourse to the law, and no legal means of preventing the attacker from striking again.

- Use the law. Whatever its inadequacies, it remains the only means of getting the aggressor behind bars.

CHAPTER 8

Protecting Your Children

Children are especially vulnerable to attack, and there can be few parents who don't worry about how best they can protect their children from harm. Children have little conception of danger, and one of the joys of a happy childhood is that freedom from the fear we learn through experience in later life.

While we should never deprive our children of their fearlessness, it is essential that we teach them to be aware of danger, and provide them with a set of family rules which protect without smothering them. Short of keeping your child locked away, there's nothing that will guarantee his or her safety. The risks will always be there.

What you can do as a parent is reduce those risks very substantially, by teaching your child how to protect him- or herself. While many of the techniques have already been discussed in the earlier chapters, it makes sense to reiterate and enlarge upon them with special reference to the young.

Recognising the danger

Many parents find it hard to believe that anyone could harm their child. Contemplating the dreadful possibilities becomes too uncomfortable, and they therefore refuse to even think about the problem.

The first thing you can do for your child is recognise that there is danger out there, and find practical measures to fight it.

Establishing a set of 'rules'

Rules for your child's self-protection should never be laid down arbitrarily. You want your child to understand the importance of these rules and adopt them willingly – not rebel against them. And you must therefore discuss and explain them as a family, not lay them down in a dictatorial fashion. This applies especially with teenagers.

As soon as your children begin to have a life independent of yours (and this may simply mean starting nursery school), they need to learn to look after themselves. You are no longer with them all of the time, protecting them from danger.

Basic rules for children

It can be hard to alert an innocent toddler to the perils of the outside world, but it is possible to do this without being alarmist. Small children can be very matter-of-fact, and the secret is to explain some basic rules to them in a simple manner.

KIDSCAPE, an organisation set up to protect children, has developed the following ten-point code. Children have a right:

1. **To be safe.** Teach children that everyone has rights, such as the right to breathe, which should not be taken away. Tell children that no one should take away their right to be safe.

2. **To protect their own bodies.** Children need to know that their bodies belong to them, particularly the private parts covered by their swimsuits.

3. **To say no.** Tell children it's all right to say 'no' to anyone if that person tries to harm them. Most children are taught to listen to and obey adults and older people without question.

4. **To get help against bullies.** Tell children to enlist the help of friends or say 'no' without fighting – and to tell an adult. Bullies are cowards, and a firm loud 'no' from a group of children with the threat of adult intervention often puts them off. In cases of real physical danger, children often have no choice but to surrender to the bully's demand.

Sometimes children will fight and get hurt to protect a possession because of the fear of what will happen when they arrive home without it. Tell them that keeping themselves safe is the most important consideration.

5. **To tell.** Assure your children that, no matter what happens, you will not be angry with them and that you want them to tell you of any incident. Children can also be very protective of parents and might not tell about a frightening occurrence because they are worried about your feelings.

6. **To be believed.** When children are told to go to an adult for help, they need to know they will be believed and supported. Although sometimes an immediate reaction is to say, 'I told you so', this will not help the child to resolve the problem. It could also prevent the child from seeking help another time. This is especially true in the case of sexual assault, as children very rarely lie about it. If the child is not believed when he or she tells, the abuse may continue for years and result in suffering and guilt for the child.

7. **To not to keep secrets.** Teach children that some secrets should NEVER be kept, no matter if they promised not to tell. Child molesters known to the child often say that a kiss or touch is 'our secret'. This confuses the child who has been taught always to keep secrets.

8. **To refuse touches.** Explain to children that they can say 'yes' or 'no' to touches or kisses from anyone, but that no one should ask them to keep touching a secret. Children sometimes do not want to be hugged or kissed, but that should be a matter of choice, not fear. They should not be forced to hug or kiss anyone.

9. **To not talk to strangers.** It is *never* a good idea to talk to a stranger. Since most well-meaning adults or teenagers do not approach children who are by themselves (unless the child is obviously lost or in distress), teach children to ignore any such approach. Children do not have to be rude. They can pretend not to hear and quickly walk or run away.

Tell children you will never be angry with them for refusing to talk to strangers and that you want to know if a stranger ever talks to them.

10. **To break rules.** Tell your children that they have your permission to break all rules to protect themselves, and tell them you will always support them if they must break a rule to stay safe. For example, it is all right to run away, to yell and create a fuss, even to lie or kick to get away from danger.

For further information on security for children, contact KIDSCAPE. Their address is listed in the Useful Addresses section on page 137.

Additional rules for teenagers

While they are stronger and – generally – more 'streetwise' than small children, their greater independence combined with their natural rebelliousness can make teenagers more vulnerable than their young brothers and sisters.

Any 'rule' *must* be discussed and explained. If your son or daughter thinks you're being unreasonable in your demands, try to get them to see your point of view. Be firm but flexible, and show you are willing to listen. Try to strike a balance between keeping your child safe and allowing him or her the freedom to grow up. And be clear about the consequences of breaking rules that have been agreed by both of you.

- Tell your son or daughter that you must always know where they are, and how you can contact them.
- Tell them that they can ring you at any time if they need your help – whatever situation they find themselves in. Your prime concern is their safety, and it's important they know you will come and fetch them – no questions asked – if they're in a situation that alarms them (e.g. a party that has got out of hand).
- Tell them they should never accept lifts from strangers.
- Tell them to trust their instincts about people – if someone makes them feel uncomfortable, they should keep away from that person, even if it means being rude.

- Tell them that you want to know about anything unpleasant that happens to them. Explain that you will not blame or punish them, and that you'd be more upset if you discovered they'd kept an incident hidden from you. Explain that these things can happen to people of all ages, and that it is *never* their fault.
- All children should be taught how to call the police (999).

Rules for specific situations

There are four situations that are worth looking at in closer detail, as they present specific, everyday dangers.

At home

Chapter 3 has already discussed ways of protecting yourself at home, and you can apply much of this material to the protection of your child. The following points are especially relevant to children:

- Don't play outside your home after dark.
- Don't tell strangers where you live.
- If you're on your own at home and someone rings the doorbell check who it is through the spyhole. If it's a stranger, **do not open the door,** even if he says that he's got an appointment with your mother or father, or that he's come to read the gas meter, or that his pregnant wife is in the car and he needs to use a phone. If you do not know him, don't let him in. No strangers should ever enter the house when your parents are out, however 'legitimate' they claim to be.
- If the person persists and frightens you, do not hesitate to call the police (999).
- Do not reveal that you're alone.

Out and about on foot

Your children should be made aware of the basic streetwise techniques supplied in Chapter 2, as well as the following points:

- If you're being followed, head straight for a friend's house (if it's nearer than your own) or a public place, like a shop. Don't try to shake off the person by taking a short cut or a route you may not know so well. Don't go home if you know there's nobody there. Try and get a good look at the man, so that you can describe him to the police.
- Wherever possible, go out with friends and return home in a group – there's safety in numbers, especially after dark.
- Try to arrange lifts with friends and family, where possible, instead of walking. And never take the risk of returning home on your own after dark.

Transport

Again, you should apply to your children the measures suggested earlier in this book, this time in Chapter 5. They should also be given some additional rules:

- Do not travel alone on public transport after dark. Arrange for a lift from your parents or friends, or take a *licensed* taxi.
- Never ride in minicabs.
- If someone is meeting you at a station, telephone and confirm the arrangement before you catch the train or bus.
- Do not accept lifts from strangers.
- Do not accept a lift from anyone who's been drinking heavily – even if it is the parent of a friend. Telephone your parents, or a taxi. (Parents: explain that you will always pay at the other end – it's a good safety valve for your child.)

As a parent you should always check with your teenager what transport arrangements have been made if they're going out in the evening. If you're at all concerned, you should be prepared to ferry them there and back – the inconvenience is compensated for by the reduction in anxiety.

Jobs

As children get older they often take on part-time jobs – newspaper rounds, working in a shop, etc. There is no reason why that job should threaten the child's safety, so long as basic precautions are taken.

- By preference jobs should be found through family and friends.
- If your child answers an advertisement, be wary, and try to go along with them when they first meet the potential employer. If they're unhappy about this, suggest they go with a friend who can wait for them outside during the interview. Don't be afraid to say 'NO' if you feel uncomfortable. Discuss your worries openly as a family.
- If your son or daughter does a paper round, teach them to refuse (politely) any invitation into a home – even if it's the home of someone they've come to know through their job.
- Always know where your child is working, and how you can contact them. Tell them you will always come and collect them if they need your help or feel threatened.
- Tell your child that if they feel uneasy or in danger they should leave the job – you won't be disappointed in them or angry.

Self-defence

In Chapter 6 I discussed a number of self-defence strategies, and all of these can be applied to children. Sit down with your son or daughter and talk about the techniques described – teach them that if someone tries to hurt them, they have every right to do whatever they can to escape from that person. This could include employing some of the fighting tactics described in the Appendix – discuss them and practise them with your children.

If your child is attacked

Your child may not tell you that he or she has been attacked – perhaps they disobeyed you by being out in the first place. However, victims of assault react in a number of ways (discussed in Chapter 7), and there will be signals for you to pick up: weeping, insomnia, obsessive washing, uncharacteristically bad behaviour, drunkenness and any other extreme behaviour.

An attack can come in many forms – your child may have been bullied at school, followed home by a stranger, fondled in the bus or sexually assaulted. Whatever the nature of the attack, once your child tells you about it, you must believe him or her and help the process of recovery.

- Tell your child that what happened to them was not their fault (victims of all ages are subject to feelings of guilt).
- Be affectionate and loving, but don't smother the child.
- By all means take your child to a doctor and the police – but be considerate of their feelings. Don't bully them, and give them time.
- If the attack was severe, suggest counselling – but again, talk this through, and don't force it on your son or daughter.
- Don't clamp down on your child's freedom – wrapping them in cotton wool will not help them recover.
- Don't make the assault taboo – make it easy for your child to talk about it with you.
- Don't be alarmed if your child does go through a difficult period – be prepared to seek help from counsellors and your doctor if you are worried.
- Be kind to yourself – you are bound to feel guilty, and a serious attack may put all sorts of stresses on the family. Understand that this is quite normal, and be prepared to seek outside help if you are worried.

If your child has been sexually assaulted by someone in your family, the trauma is often worse. Remember that if your child tells you that they have suffered in this way, **he or she is most unlikely to be lying** – this is not easy information for any child to give away. The following steps are recommended if you are faced with this terrible situation:

- Try to ensure the offence is never repeated – try to keep

your child's life as normal as possible, but protect them from being left alone with the assailant.

- Confront the assailant, either on your own or with someone you trust – *believe your child*, whatever the assailant says.
- Whatever your feelings about the offender (he may be a husband or father whom you love), your responsibility is to your child. **Do not protect the offender, protect the child.**
- Call the police if the assailant becomes violent – whatever your relationship with him. Again, you must always bear in mind the safety and welfare of your child.
- Seek help from one of the agencies listed in Useful Addresses.

Summary

The intention of this final chapter is to help mothers help their children to protect themselves. All families are different, and you will need to develop a protection strategy that suits your circumstances and your children. Across the board, however, the basic rules apply:

- Recognise that the world is a dangerous place – your child needs to learn the rules of self-protection.

- Establish a set of family rules.

- Discuss these with your child – especially if he or she is a teenager. Avoid laying down the law in an arbitrary fashion.

- Be prepared to listen to your children and show them that your concern in their safety – not the curtailment of their freedom.

- Discuss and practise the self-defence strategies outlined in Chapter 6 and Appendix.

- If your child tells you they've been attacked, **believe them** and follow the steps suggested in this chapter.

Books, Booklets and Videos

Pauline Bart and Patricia O'Brien, *Stopping Rape – Successful Survival Strategies* (Pergamon £11)

Ian Blair, *Investigating Rape – A new approach for police* (The Police Foundation)

Denise Caignon and Gail Groves, *Her Wits About Her* (The Women's Press £5.95)

Anne Dickson, *A Woman In Your Own Right – Assertiveness And You* (Quartet £3.95)

Michele Elliott, *Keeping Safe: A Practical Guide to Talking With Children* (New English Library/Hodder & Stoughton £2.99)

Health and Safety Executive booklet, *Preventing Violence to Staff* (HMSO £3.95)

Diana Lamplugh, *Beating Aggression: A Practical Guide for Working Women* (Weidenfeld and Nicholson £5.95)

NSPCC booklet, *Protect Your Child* (free)

Simon Romain, *How to Live Safely in a Dangerous World* (Robson £8.95)

Ann Sedley and Melissa Benn, *Sexual Harassment at Work* (Liberty – formerly NCCL – 95p)

Police and Home Office publications

Positive Action – Guidance on safety and self-defence for women (free booklet) Video also available

Positive Steps – Help and advice for women on personal safety (free booklet from police) Video also available

Practical Ways to Crack Crime – the Family Guide (free booklet)

Violent Crime – Police advice for women on how to reduce the risks (free booklet)

Videos

Avoiding Danger, available from NACAB Vision, 115–123 Pentonville Road, London N1 9LZ (Price £30)

Make a success of Neighbourhood Watch, available from your local Crime Prevention Officer or CFL Vision, PO Box 35, Wetherby, Yorks LS23 7EX; 0937 541010

KIDSCAPE Primary Kit (pack includes posters, leaflets, teaching manuals), available from *KIDSCAPE*, address supplied opposite (Price £45 plus £2.50 p&p)

Positive Steps, available from Cygnet Films, Bilton Centre Studios, Coronation Road, High Wycombe, Buckinghamshire; 0494 450541

Useful Addresses

Age Concern (supply help and advice on security matters for the elderly) 081–640 5431

Automobile Association (AA) Head Office: Fanum House, Basingstoke, Hants RG21 2EA; 0256 20123

Childline (confidential advice for children) Freepost 1111, London N1 0BR; 0800 1111

Criminal Injuries Compensation Board 19 Alfred Place, London WC1E 7EJ; 071–636 9501

Driving Management Limited Audubon House, Bradcutts Lane, Cookham Dean, Berks SL6 9AA; 06285 27387

Health and Safety Executive 21 offices nationwide. For your local office contract Baynards House, 1 Chepstow Place, Westbourne Grove, London W2 4TF; 071–221 0870

KIDSCAPE World Trade Centre, Europe House, Box No 10, London E1 9AA; 071–488 0488

Ladycabs 071–254 3501

Matrix 071–249 7603

Mothers of Abused Children 0965 31432

Network 071–274 4000 × 249

NSPCC 67 Saffron Hill, London EC1N 8RS; 071–242 1626

Parents Anonymous 071–263 8918

Rape Crisis Centres Either see local telephone directory, or phone 071–837 1600 or 031–556 9437 (for Scotland) for the nearest centre

Redwood Women's Training Association (assertiveness training courses available nationwide) Redwood, Invergarry, Kitlings Lane, Walton on the Hill, Stafford ST17 0LE; 0785 662823

Rights of Women (free legal advice for women by female lawyers) 071–251 6577

Royal Automobile Club (RAC) Head Office: PO Box 100, RAC House, Lansdowne Road, Croydon; 081–686 2525

Samaritans Your local number will be listed in the directory; 24–hour counselling service for anybody

Suzy Lamplugh Trust 14 East Sheen Avenue, London SW14 8AS; 081–392 1839

Transport User Consultative Committees
London: 071–839 1898
Scotland: 041–221 7760
Wales: 0222 227247
Eastern District: 0733 312188
The Midlands: 021–643 2144
The North East: 0904 625615
The North West: 061–228 6247
Western District: 0272 265703
Southern District (excluding London): 071–839 1851

Victim Support Schemes (support and help to victims) For your local branch contact head office at Cranmer House, 39 Brixton Road, London SW9 6DZ; 071–735 9166

WASH (Women Against Sexual Harassment) 071–833 0777

WAVAW (Women Against Violence Against Women) 071–923 1374

Women's Design Service 071–241 6910

Index

APPENDIX

Practical Ways to Defend Yourself

This book has shown the many ways in which you can avoid violent physical confrontation with an attacker. In every situation, your priority must be to preempt or deflect violence, and getting into a fight must always be your last resort.

If you do have to fight, you must fight dirty. Your aim is to inflict extreme localised pain on the aggressor so that he is forced to release you – if only for a brief moment. During that moment you flee. Don't look back, and don't be tempted to administer that extra kick.

Most women are unused to fighting. Unlike boys, we haven't learned the tactics in playground and pub brawls, and most of us shy away from the thought of physically hurting somebody else. This is a principal reason for the passivity of so many women when attacked.

If we are to protect ourselves, we have to revise our attitudes to violence NOW. Sometimes it is a necessary evil, the only way in which a victim of attack can save her life. If you are not committed to hurting your aggressor, he will prevail.

It is against the law to carry firearms, knives or other weapons – even a sharpened metal comb carried in your pocket would be viewed unfavourably in court. However, there are many 'weapons' you can carry quite legitimately and which can be invaluable in the face of violence. A hairspray, a bunch of keys, an umbrella or walking stick, a screech alarm: all these can be used to hurt an aggressor, and give you that brief advantage which allows you to escape.

The tactics shown on the following pages are for use against an *unarmed* attacker. If he is carrying a knife or gun, there is little you can do. Fighting him is far too dangerous. Your best bet is to try and disarm him by talking and pretending you are willing to comply with his demands. The minute he does put down his weapon, strike out at him, hurt him and flee – taking the weapon with you.

You may be smaller and weaker than your aggressor, you may feel that physically you are ill-equipped to gain the advantage over him in a fight. But if you are angry and committed enough, and if you concentrate on going for his vulnerable points, you stand a very good chance of hurting him and getting away.

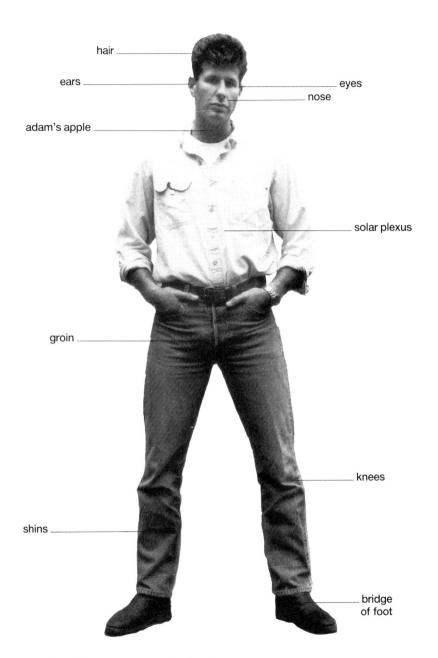

hair

ears

eyes

nose

adam's apple

solar plexus

groin

knees

shins

bridge
of foot

Sensitive parts of an attacker's body.

You may not be as strong as your attacker, but if you concentrate
on his vulnerable points, you *can* gain the advantage in a struggle.

1

2

3

Ways to escape from a man holding you round the neck from behind.

1 Grab hold of his little finger(s), and pull them back as far as you can. Be committed to breaking them.

2 Butt his nose with the back of your head.

3 Stamp hard on the bridge of his foot, using your heel. This is especially effective if you're wearing stilettos.

1

2

Further ways to escape from a man holding you from behind.

1 Swing your elbow backwards into his solar plexus.

2 Kick his knee with your heel.

3 Kick his shin with your heel.

3

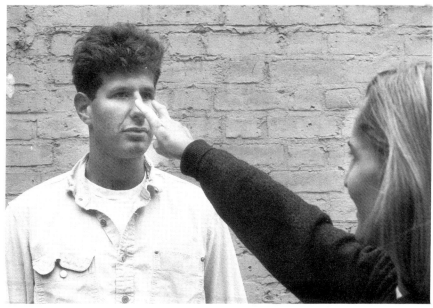

1

2

Vulnerable points on the face, and how to attack them.

1 Poke his eyes hard with your index and middle finger.

2 Grab his ears and twist them as hard as you can.

1

2

Effective blows to the face.

1 Bring the butt of your hand up hard under his nose.

2 Thump his Adam's apple with the butt of your hand.

1

2

Using your head as a weapon.

1 Pull his hair,

2 and butt his nose with your forehead at the same time.

1

2

Effective ways of kicking an attacker as he lunges towards you.

1 Never kick him in the groin with your foot – he could grab it and unbalance you. Use your knee.

2 If you kick with your foot, aim for the shin.

3 Alternatively, you can swing round and do a back kick with your heel, aiming for his knee.

3

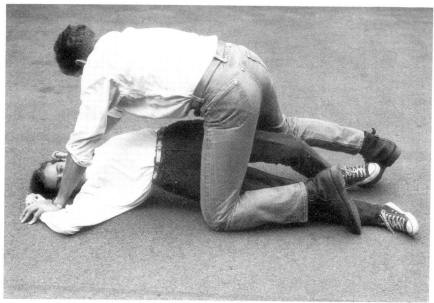

1

2

How to escape from a man who has you pinned to the ground and is sitting astride you.

1 Twist your hip to one side . . .

2 and as he loses his balance, bite the soft underside of his wrist;

3

4

3 as he releases your hand, hit him hard under his nose with the butt of your fist, and . . .

4 flee.

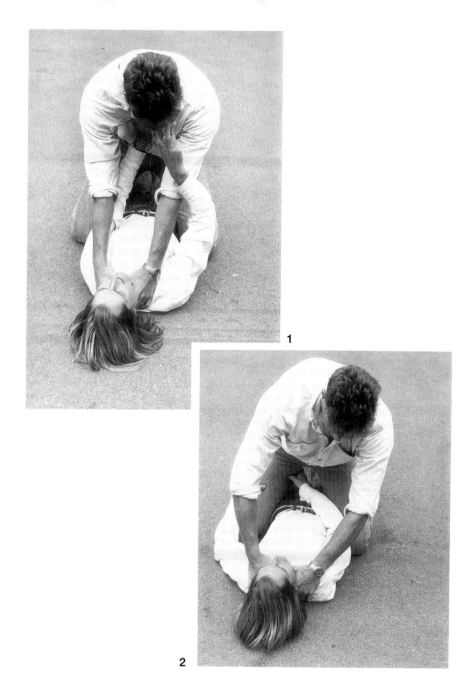

1

2

How to escape from an attacker who is throttling you as you lie on the ground.

1 Your hands are free, so use one to poke his eyes.

2 Bring the other hand up between his legs, and whack him hard in the groin or squeeze his thigh hard.

1

2

The photographs from this page onwards illustrate ways in which you can turn everyday objects into weapons for self-defence. Here we deal with bunches of keys, splayed between fingers.

1 Punch him in the face with your fist and keys.

2 Punch the back of his hand (if he grabs you from behind).

1

2

Using screech alarm or hair lacquer on an attacker.

1 Set off your screech alarm in his ear.

2 Spray hair lacquer in his eyes.

Ways of turning a briefcase into a weapon.

1 If you're carrying a briefcase, swing it upwards and whack him hard in the groin.

2 Alternatively, grab it between both hands and use it to hit his Adam's apple as hard as possible.

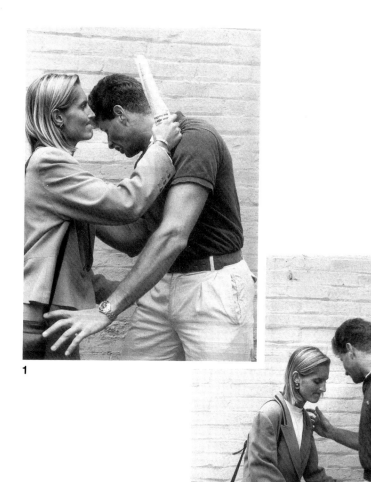

1

2

Even a newspaper or magazine can be turned into an effective weapon.

1 Beat him hard on the ears, or . . .

2 hit him as hard as you can between the legs.

1

2

The following defensive techniques are especially relevant for elderly people with walking sticks.

1 If he grabs you from behind, you can use your brolly or walking stick to jab him in the solar plexus.

2 If he's lunging towards you, a similar tactic is applied.

1 Whack him hard with stick or umbrella on the side of his knee.

2 Whack him hard on the wrists.